THE MERCURY MIND

How Harnessing Attraction Beyond Your Control is
the Key to Better Relationships, Fulfilling Careers,
and Your Most Powerful Self

NATHAN LANCRY

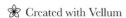

Thank you to the relationships of my past, and words cannot describe my gratitude for the beautiful people in my life presently.

Contents

Introduction: Relationships Matter More than we Think

It's hard to find anyone who will deny that relationships are important in our lives. But few of us realize just how much they truly matter. Relationships are *powerful*. They can open us up to the limitless potential within ourselves or burn us down to a hollow husk. We have all heard examples of people performing superhuman feats to save a loved one's life, or a husband passing away days after his wife dies.

Science bears out that relationships can raise us up or tear us down. As social creatures, bonding to others is in our genes and is vital to our survival. Being rejected by a social group causes pain and spurs us to find a more accepting group that can help us weather tough winters and brutal summers. For our early ancestors, inclusion in a tribe meant we had resources when we needed aid. As a result, meaningful relationships are literally good for our health. They can even give us superhero strength.

When Angela Cavallo heard the crash, she knew something was terribly wrong.[1] As she ran outside, she saw her sixteen-year-old son, Tony, pinned underneath his 1964 Chevy Impala. She didn't think, she acted. She lifted the car four inches off of her son's unconscious body while a neighbor ran to get help. She was not going to let her son die shortly after being able to grow his first mustache. Miraculously, Tony survived with no brain damage, all because of the power of his mother's love.

After the incident, Cavallo became a legend, the poster woman who proved moms could be superheroes. But Angela's case isn't unique. The phenomenon of "hysterical strength" has been documented several times, from the Canadian woman who fought off a polar bear to defend her children[2] to the woman behind the inspiration for the Hulk.[3]

Intense love can make our bodies capable of seemingly impossible feats. The body is not separate from the emotions, but an extension of them. Our search for authentic, meaningful, and healthy connections is not simply a matter of emotional well-being. When we embrace what we truly want and act with integrity from a place of love, we strengthen ourselves physically and mentally, and can accomplish things we thought were impossible.

But while healthy relationships can lift us up, even mildly unhealthy relationships can bring us down. We might recognize this when a friend starts a new job, excited about being able to contribute in a new workplace. But over the course of a month, we see his usually boisterous nature become more subdued. We hear at work his new boss has shut down many of his ideas and so he's stopped contributing, knowing he'll receive a "No" in response. Our friend is physically healthy, and isn't necessarily depressed or anxious, but he's...different. He's less himself since he started his new job.

Sometimes the relationships we chase turn out to be wrong for us. We killed ourselves in medical school because we chose a mentor who wouldn't settle for anything other than perfection. We love our go-getter partner, but we wish she would spend at least a weekend or two a month at home. We told ourselves for years we wanted lots of children, but as we settle on the couch with our toddlers to watch Peppa Pig for the millionth time, we long for our pre-kid freedom. As the excitement from achieving our relationship goals subsides, we realize our lives haven't gotten any better. And sometimes, these relationships leave us worse off than before.

Take, for example, the case of Renee Linell.[4] Renee felt like an outcast most of her life. At thirty-three, she wandered into a tantric meditation class with a young, lively instructor in stiletto heels, who took the students on a meditation journey using techno music. Renee was enchanted, by the class, the attendees, and her instructor. This group of people seemed like the perfect fit for her and she worked hard to be accepted into the social circle.

After a few years, however, this music haven turned into a discordant hell. With a gaslighting leader driving the bus of her new social group, Renee began to doubt herself. She relinquished financial assets to the group, cut off communication to friends and family, and entered into a sexual relationship with the head guru. After seven years, she was agoraphobic, anorexic, exhausted, and deeply depressed. It wasn't until a near-death experience that Renee was able to clear away the fog surrounding her relationships and re-examine what she truly wanted.

Unhealthy relationships can devolve further into abuse and are linked with a suite of mental health problems like depression, PTSD, and a propensity toward self-harm.[5] Moreover, these situations can bring about long-term physical consequences. According to the U.S. Department of Health and Human Services, this includes conditions like migraines, heart conditions, digestive issues, asthma, immunological deficiencies, and even arthritis.[6] One study found abuse victims had a 49% greater chance of suffering cancer later in life![7]

A relationship doesn't need to cross into full-on abuse to be detrimental to our health. Even unhealthy relationships that are ill-matched with who we are and what we want out of life can have dire consequences. For example, data collected from the famous Whitehall II study of nearly 30,000 participants found a strong correlation between toxic work relationships and health problems such as heart disease, high BMI, high blood pressure, and nicotine addiction.[8]

Any unhealthy relationship can produce chronic stress, which comes with complications. For example, one study found couples who reported more marital stress had higher blood pressure.[9] Another study shows that while people in good relationships have on average better mental health than their single counterparts, people in turbulent relationships have worse mental well-being than their solo pals.[10]

Even relationships that aren't explicitly unhealthy can have negative consequences. For example, if others in your network have unhealthy habits, the chances are good you will adopt some negative behaviors as well. One study that took place over the course of three decades assessed how weight gain in one person affected family, friends, and romantic partners.[11] If one spouse was obese, there was a 37 percent higher likelihood their partner would be too. If one sibling was overweight, the chances of their brother or sister becoming rotund increased by 40 percent. And if a friend was portly, the odds of having a large waistline shot up by 57 percent.

In light of all of the distressing repercussions of unhealthy relationships, it may be tempting to believe loneliness is better than involvement with a toxic partner. However, the science shows loneliness is just as harmful to our health as unhealthy relationships, if not more.

When we isolate ourselves, our health takes a toll. Research suggests social isolation is a predictor of social media addiction, which comes with a host of side effects including low self-esteem and decreased ability to focus.[12] Further studies show the human need for bonding and intimacy can lead socially isolated individuals to manufacture the feeling of bonding through excessive opioid use.[13] And perhaps the most well known analysis of social isolation equates chronic loneliness with smoking 15 cigarettes per day. Anxiety and depression, the off-shoots of rejection, are linked with long-term illnesses such as cancer.[14] Loneliness can literally kill.

Loneliness is no better than unhealthy relationships. But we don't have to settle for one or the other. There is a reason we find ourselves cycling in and out of satisfying relationships and checking boxes but feeling unfulfilled at the same time.

It's not that we don't have any good friends, loving partners, or friendly work relationships. Rather, we all have some connections in our lives but we know those bonds could be deeper, richer, and more fulfilling. Maybe we have a colleague we'd like to work with more. Or perhaps we've drifted away from our sister and we'd like to rebuild the bond we once had in our youth. Or it could be that we love our partner of five years, but we'd like to deepen the connection as we move forward into the next five.

We don't want relationships that only look good on paper, we want meaningful bonds. We want deep connections. And it turns out there is a science behind these powerful, authentic relationships. We can reverse engineer the process of developing incredibly deep connections with others. But, paradoxically, the key to getting there lies to letting go of our conscious plans. We can't connect with others on this level until we can connect with our own deep inner truth. And that's a lot harder than it seems.

Good Relationships Save Us

In the case of Donna Davies, love literally saved her life.[15] After years of sexual abuse from a family friend, she fell into a deep depression. Although she eventually reported the abuse and the perpetrator was jailed, Donna still felt aimless, isolated, and purposeless. She began slowly killing herself through overdoses, cutting, and even injecting bleach into her skin. This self-abuse landed her in a hospital several times between the ages of thirteen and nineteen.

At nineteen, after a severe allergic reaction from injecting white spirit into her arm, Donna was on the brink of death. Her recovery was long and tortuous. Her few blurry thoughts were dedicated to the best ways of killing herself as soon as she was released. Then, a surprise visitor came in the door. Her old friend Michael poked his head into her room and, for what seemed like the first time in years she actually felt seen. They connected and, as they did, she suddenly wanted to go for walks. Over time, she felt her vitality return, her hope revitalize, and her very will to live come back. She wanted to be a better woman for this man. She recovered physically and mentally because of her love for Michael.

It wasn't something that happened in an instant. It wasn't a quick-fix cure. It was years of friendship and trust in the making that built a relationship that could stand up to Donna's demons. When the story came to light, Donna and Michael were married with a child on the way. It proves an enduring deep connection is powerful enough to make a seemingly incurably sick woman step back from death's door and into life's waiting arms.

While the impact of deep connection is certainly powerful, many may make the mistake of believing this type of relationship has only temporary neurological and mental impacts. For years, psychologists believed the term limit for romantic love was between eighteen months to three years[16]. If this was the case, the long-term effects of a deep connection would be negligible. However, this is not the case. Research has been conducted on couples married an average of twenty-one years who were purportedly still madly in love with their partners. Their brain scans showed stimulation in regions associated with dopamine production, obsession, sexual attraction, and long-term attachments.[17] These patterns are not only consistent with data from newly-in-love couples, but from long-term attachments as well. In other words, a deep connection that lasts bears the hallmarks of both the insanity of new love and the stability of long-term bonding. It is possible to get the best of both worlds.

A long-lasting deep connection doesn't only confer the exciting benefits of new love, it also has the calming security of lasting connection on our mind and body. After we've been with someone for one or two years of blissful union we experience a drop in cortisol[2] and a rise in oxytocin and vasopressin, which creates feelings of secure attachment instead of stress. Studies show couples in long-term partnerships have lower blood pressure,[18] between 7-12% decreased risk of vascular disease,[19] better overall mental well-being, and higher self-esteem.[20]

Additionally, long-term love can actually help us to survive. A 2011 meta-analysis of ninety-five studies with a composite of 500 million participants conclusively demonstrated early mortality was much higher in single than in married individuals—by almost twenty-four percent in some studies![21] In another 2012 study, married coronary bypass patients were 2.5 times more likely to survive than their single counterparts.[22] This number jumped even further when the participants reported being *happily* married.

These benefits are not restricted to romantic connections, either. Networks of strong familial, friendship, and work relationships have been associated with longevity. In fact, a 2010 meta-analysis found a good network of relationships increased survivability by fifty percent.[23] By comparison, this means positive relationships are as beneficial in reducing your mortality risk as quitting smoking, and twice as advantageous as regular physical activity. But the benefits don't stop there. Good ties also lower blood pressure[24], weight, and even the risk of dementia.[25]

Good relationships also build high self-esteem, allowing us to express our authentic selves with a greater level of confidence. This is why research demonstrates a definitive link between authenticity and self-esteem.[26] Consequently, behaving from a place of high authenticity is correlated with better overall health, more successful goal attainment, lower stress, and greater levels of happiness and optimism. Healthy relationships give us everything most of us truly want out of life. The answer is as easy as dedicating our lives to cultivating real, honest love.

Purposeful relationships can help us live healthy, happy lives. This is not simply a matter of becoming a little more satisfied with ourselves, or having a relationship that scores a nine out of ten instead of a six out of ten. It can quite literally make the difference between life and death.

When we enable ourselves with tools to pursue our authentic wants and create a pathway toward healthy relationships and high self-esteem, we are actively deciding to *live a high-quality, meaningful existence*, not just in the spiritual or philosophical sense, but in a concrete, physical way.

In this book, we'll see how to identify our attractions and come to accept them as they are. We'll explore proven methods to test whether our actions are in line with our long term goals, or if we're self-sabotaging to preserve a conscious attraction over an authentic subconscious desire. We'll look at some ways to become more comfortable with ourselves and build on self-esteem instead of self-confidence, so we can perpetuate ourselves towards satisfaction in all facets of life. But first, we have to explore the biggest issue that often holds us back from truly meaningful relationships: we don't even know what will actually make us happy.

We Don't Know what
We Want

We all want more Mercury Mind connections in our lives. When a friend turns redder than an apple telling us about her 48-hour-long first date, we can surmise she might be at the beginning of a Mercury Mind connection. When our partner skips off to work an hour early because he wants to catch up on the office gossip with his "work husband," we might recognize another Mercury Mind connection. And when we witness someone double over in laughter at the same joke their partner has been telling for the past twenty-five years, we know there is a Mercury Mind Connection between them. If you've ever met someone for the first time and had the bizarre feeling that you've known them forever, you have experienced an incipient Mercury Mind Connection.

The strange thing about this type of electric connection is that it's impossible to plan for. We think we know what we want, but we aren't always right. We think the perfect partner will be a certain height, have a certain job, and share certain interests. But then we meet someone completely different who blows us away. We interview dozens of candidates for the job opening and none of them seem quite right, despite matching all of our criteria. Then we talk with someone totally out-of-the-box who we immediately know is the perfect fit.

Most of us could sit down and spend all day listing exactly what we want out of our relationships. We might specify that we crave a romantic partner who makes us laugh and works out as much as we do. We can describe ideal interactions with our colleagues, bosses, and employees. We may dream of finding a group of friends in which we feel simultaneously unique and part of a squad.

Except sometimes we do find a boss, partner, or friends who tick all of our boxes, yet, we don't feel as good as we thought we would. The self-conscious high schooler finally gets accepted by the popular kids only to find being part of the in crowd doesn't bring pure bliss. The awkward accountant eventually wins the attention of the beautiful barista but doesn't feel he's living happily ever after like he imagined he would. The disgruntled employee secures a new job with a perfect boss only to discover she still gets stressed out and bored with the monotonous tasks.

It seems odd that our well thought-out lists of the qualities we are looking for in other people don't lead directly to satisfying relationships. Why do we often get it wrong? The problem turns out to be much deeper than it seems…

The Mercury Mind

Mercury is one of the most curious substances on the periodic table. It is the only metal that is liquid at room temperature. Like water, it can take any shape, yet mercury would rather bind to itself. On its own it forms perfectly round silver beads. If two beads of mercury come in contact, they will instantly form one larger bead, which is also perfectly round. Mercury is the most malleable metal. It can easily bond with other elements. However, most of these pairings are highly toxic.

People work in a similar way. We can form bonds with others, but when we shape-shift to fit into someone else's mold, the situation can become toxic. It's not that we need to enter into relationships with people who are just like us. Rather, we need to find those connections that allow us to be our authentic selves.

Unhealthy relationships are often a result of trying to make our Mercury Minds bond to elements that don't reflect our true selves. In order to have healthy relationships we must tap into our authentic truth. When we are genuinely ourselves, we naturally find more stable, rewarding relationships. We attract other people who are connected to their authentic selves too. These relationships are known as Mercury Mind connections.

When we first meet someone we feel a Mercury Mind connection to, it is akin to true "attraction", as sociologist Helen Fisher termed it.[1] This type of connection is marked by high levels of dopamine and norepinephrine, and low levels of serotonin, the combination of which makes us feel as if we could do anything, but also as if we are walking on a glass floor that threatens to shatter with every step. We are motivated to nurture the relationship, and yet we remain cautious, afraid to mess things up.

The trouble, of course, is that Mercury Mind connections do not always turn into healthy relationships. When we are newly attracted to a person, our bodies repress the functioning of our amygdala and frontal lobe, the parts of our body that control decisioning-making and threat responses.[2] In other words, we generally become worse decision makers in the beginning stages of a relationship and systematically ignore the red flags waving in the breeze. This is why our friend won't listen when we suggest her new beau with the cocaine addiction is bad news.

These lapses in judgment can lead us down the path of ignoring what we truly want in order to secure the relationship. It is often easier to see the red flags from the outside when someone we know is love-drunk. We recognize our friend's boss is toxic, but our friend is smitten with how cool they are. We realize our mom's employee is taking advantage of her kindness, but mom ignores it because the employee is young and "just needs some guidance." We see our coworker's boyfriend guilting her for money, but she dismisses the observation because he brings her flowers "just because."

Often we gravitate toward unhealthy relationships without discretion because there is something about the relationship that we consciously want. However, pursuit of our conscious plans without listening to our authentic desires gets us into trouble and can lead to toxic relationships. If we can tap into our authentic desires and detach from our conscious plans, then we will have a greater chance of forming Mercury Mind connections, or relationships that nourish rather than drain us.

If you think you've experienced a Mercury Mind connection, only to have the relationship disintegrate into name-calling, passive-aggressive maneuvers, or outright malevolence, likely you have been caught in the crosshairs of conflicting conscious plans and subconscious authentic desires.

Conscious vs. Authentic Attractions

When we double-down on relationships that appear to check our boxes, but are not in line with our authentic desires, the results can be detrimental to our physical, mental, and emotional health. So why is it that we continue to cycle in and out of unfulfilling relationships? Because our conscious plans and authentic desires are in conflict.

Conscious attractions are the dreams we articulate when someone asks us what our ten year goals are. For example, we might want a house in Beverly Hills, sculpted triceps, the latest Tesla, or TikTok fame. We may genuinely want these things, and be willing to work hard to obtain them, but, when we analyze these a bit closer, they are often representative of a subconscious authentic desire.

Authentic attractions are our genuine desires. They are indicative of who we truly are and wish to be, independent of what society and others may think. Authentic desires are often subconscious, shadowing the person we think we should be, and tripping him up in an attempt to be more fully seen. They usually underlie our conscious attractions.

The trouble is that our subconscious genuine attractions are usually vague. They aren't neatly underlined with clearly defined milestones like conscious attractions are. We usually prefer conscious attractions over our subconscious ones because they appear more tangible. They are easier to define, contend with, and accomplish through our actions, even if they ultimately leave us feeling dissatisfied. If we consciously want to sleep with a new partner every night, but feel drained after a handful of one-night-stands, our subconscious authentic desire might be intimacy. If we consciously crave national fame, but feel awkward recording TikToks, our subconscious attraction beneath the surface might be admiration from our peers. If we consciously desire a house in Beverly Hills, the genuine attraction may be long-term financial security for our family. Intimacy, admiration from peers, and financial stability are more difficult to define and achieve compared to racking up ten notches in our bedposts, thirty-thousand TikTok followers, or an address in Beverly Hills.

Further, our authentic desires are difficult to identify because we have suppressed them for so long. If our subconscious attractions are taboo according to our social circle, cultural identity, and society at large, we usually learn at a young age to sequester them away in dark corners of our hearts. We push them deep down in an attempt to avoid rejection and feelings of guilt or shame, and become so used to doing so, we have trouble consciously admitting to them.

But our subconscious genuine attractions are like a cork in water. No matter how hard we try to suppress our authentic desires, they still bob up. The cork, like a genuine attraction, is naturally buoyant and will always float to the surface no matter how deep it is submerged.

Consider the life of Cleopatra. The fourth century empress Cleopatra VII is famous for her attractions to military power, political prowess, and indulgent romances with influential men like Julius Caesar and Mark Antony, but underneath her seemingly power-hungry behaviors a subconscious desire persists in bobbing up. Cleopatra may have consciously sought power, but her conscious plans chafed against her authentic attraction toward belonging.

Cleopatra was not Egyptian by blood. Her ancestry was, in fact, Macedonian. But in an attempt to gain power, respect, and belonging in a place where she was essentially a foreigner, she learned the Egyptian language and dressed in the style of an Egyptian goddess. As a supreme ruler she could have had her advisors learn the language and manage her image, yet, she took it upon herself to become more like the people she ruled.

However, this did not allow her to strengthen bonds with her family. In fact, Cleopatra's command of the Egyptian people conflicted with co-ruler, King Ptolemy XIII, her brother, and he conspired against her, forcing her to flee Egypt for her own safety. Outcast by her own family and political counsel, Cleopatra sought to bully her way back in, and raised an army to overthrow her brother and take Egypt back for herself.

It just so happened that while Cleopatra was raising her army, Julius Caesar was preparing to lay siege to Egypt and gain a foothold for his return to power in Rome. Sensing an opportunity, Cleopatra began a political and intimate relationship with Caesar and together they conquered Alexandria, and installed Cleopatra as the leader of Egypt. However, Cleopatra, having just waged war on her own people, was unpopular. A social outcast among her countrymen, she sought belonging from her relationship with Caesar and the couple had a child.

Unfortunately, Cleopatra was again left scrambling for belonging when Caesar was murdered. Recognizing that acceptance from the Egyptian populace was now near impossible, she jumped at the chance to belong to someone new. Mark Antony invited her to discuss politics and Cleopatra planned their meeting around seduction. Plutarch writes that she intentionally delayed her trip to heighten Antony's anticipation, brought gallant ships loaded with gifts for Antony, and dressed in the robes of Isis to pair her stature as a goddess with Antony's self-described image of the god Dionysus. He fell for her instantly and left his wife Fulvia and their children in Italy. The two moved to Alexandria, started a new family by having children together, and made plans to be buried together someday.

With her authentic desire for belonging finally satisfied, she was able to bring Egypt into substantial wealth and prominence. But outside forces threatened the couple's power and Antony left to reestablish his dominance and loyalty to Rome. Parted from each other, they each lost their grip on power. Antony attempted to salvage the couple's influence in Rome by declaring Cleopatra's son with

Caesar as the heir to the Roman throne, but this backfired and the couple reunited in Greece as their forces waged war against rival Roman factions.

Their conscious plan to be in power conflicted with their desire for belonging, and this ultimately led to their deaths. While on the battlefield, Antony received news that Cleopatra died and he decided to fall on his sword. In his final moments, he entered Cleopatra's mausoleum where he found Cleopatra alive, sequestered away for her own safety. Bleeding out, he begged her to make peace with Octavian before dying in her arms. Cleopatra's authentic desire to belong slipped away in front of her eyes. Instead of reaching for power, she chose to die with Antony, perhaps thinking they would be united in an afterlife. Whether or not they met again, they were ultimately buried together as they had planned.

Cleopatra's conscious attraction is clear: power. But a deeper desire for belonging drove much of her behavior as well. If she truly wanted power, she wouldn't have bothered trying to fit in as an Egyptian. If power had been her sole authentic aim, she would have cut short her romances with Caesar and Antony when their political careers first showed signs of fumbling, to preserve her status. Instead of killing herself to be with Antony in the afterlife, she could have struck a deal with Octavian and returned to rule a prosperous Egypt.

It seems odd such a clever, seductive, power-hungry leader would kill herself in a mausoleum instead of crafting a way to maintain her status as the Queen of Egypt, but her actions make sense in terms of her subconscious attraction.

We think we know what we want in life, but the truth is most of us have subconscious authentic desires working backstage, tugging on the curtain ropes, and affecting our overall experience of the show in front of us. Because of this, it might feel like no matter how hard we try, partners always break our hearts, bosses always micromanage, and our latest friend group never "gets" our sense of humor. Like Cleopatra, we often pursue new relationships with alacrity, only to watch them turn to rubble in the conflict between our conscious designs and subconscious attractions.

When we suppress our authentic desires, we bury our true selves.

This means we fail to attract Mercury Mind connections, and instead toxically meld to people who fit our conscious plans, further distancing ourselves from our genuine wants.

But the outlook is not all doom and gloom. By embracing our authentic desires and working with our Mercury Minds, we can fully embrace our genuine selves and attract healthy, fulfilling, connections.

Authentic Connections

Mercury Mind connections take place when we are in touch with our authentic desires. We may have had Mercury Mind encounters previously, but if we can't maintain our authentic personalities, these relationships deteriorate. It is effortful to nurture a connection with someone while also suppressing ourselves, and pretending to be someone we are not.

It is clear that we cannot escape our genuine desires. Despite our attempts to outrun our subconscious authentic wants, they always catch up with us. This may seem daunting, but there is nothing wrong with our desires. Our Mercury Mind cannot change what it is drawn to, and denying our authentic wants will only cause further pain. We attempt to cover up this pain using quick-fix conscious goals and surface-level relationships, which leaves us dissatisfied. Attempting to suppress parts of ourselves saddles us with the weight of maintaining a false identity.

This is tiring because it requires constant effort to resist or suppress our genuine desires. We expend energy covering our true selves up, rather than energy going after or nurturing what we truly want. We will never access true Mercury Mind relationships if we are busy posturing as someone else.

Our need to suppress our authentic desires stems from an unsteady flow of self-esteem. When we accomplish our conscious plans, we feel self-confident. *We accomplished something, we achieved success, and we are great*, we might think. But, feeling great *because of* an accomplishment is one thing. Feeling great by nature of the fact that we merely exist is an entirely different thing. Knowing we are great merely by nature of existing is also known as self esteem. Self esteem is much deeper, more authentic, and much harder to develop than self-confidence, but it is crucial to attracting and maintaining Mercury Mind connections. Plus, once we gain self-esteem, things get a whole lot easier.

If we are going to recognize our authentic desires, we will need to cultivate a steady level of self-esteem. Ultimately, the work we do to realize our subconscious desires will allow us to access that deep well of self-esteem, so that we can throw off the chains of shame and guilt that have kept our authentic selves sequestered away in dark dungeons. Stepping into the light of genuineness opens us up to attracting more Mercury Mind connections in our lives. The trick is to become comfortable exploring uncharted territory, especially the choppy waters within our own psyches. Instead of resisting the discomfort of the unknown, we must learn to embrace it.

2

Closing Uncertain Cycles

Why do we cling to our conscious desires rather than surrendering to our authentic attractions? Because humans loathe uncertainty. We would much rather believe we know exactly what we want than admit we have no idea why we are drawn to some people and repulsed by others. So we develop rationalizations to make sense of our choices. We convince ourselves we understand why one person bores us while another excites us.

The human need for certainty is not merely a philosophical conjecture, but a proven conclusion, rooted in our evolutionary history. In our species' infancy, we migrated from plains to jungles to icy tundras. With each new environment, the cultural and social mores changed along with our genes.[1] Constant migration was the norm for the first few hundred thousand years of our species' existence, so we became adept at quickly evaluating potential stressors in our environments and responding in kind. Knowing the risks provides us with protection. When we cannot predict future threats like a snowstorm, animal ambush, or depletion of vital resources, we become anxious.

In the modern world, a different kind of uncertainty assails us. Instead of the lion creeping around the corner, we face the uncertainty of our careers, our socioeconomic status, and our affiliations. In response, we conjure up easy-to-understand plans, instead of admitting we don't know exactly what we want. We might have an authentic desire to live on a commune with artists, but faced with the uncertainty of how to go about it, we go to school for accounting and turn into a grumpy CPA. Or, we may dream of marrying a woman who is a pasta connoisseur, but instead we stay with our current partner who hates carbs. We might long for a closer relationship with our brother, but, unsure of how to achieve that, we engage in frequent spats with him instead. When we don't know what we want, we rush into a solution, even if it doesn't align with our authentic desires.

When we are young, inexperienced, and insecure, our plans for the distant future repeatedly fall through. If we surveyed our peers, we'd likely notice very few of them are in careers directly related to their first collegiate degree. Of the dozens of close friends we've had in our lives, we might recall a mere handful of individuals who made their high school relationship last. We may not know a single person who set a definite course in life and stuck to it forever. When we are young, our plans fail all the time, and we have habituated to quickly committing to a new plan and wrapping up the uncertainty.

As a result of this tendency to manufacture a sense of closure where it doesn't really exist, we develop a host of false and unsatisfactory answers. And these answers will lead us back to uncertainty sooner or later. Our Mercury Minds meld into toxic relationships, which leads to chronic stress and inflammation. This is why we have more physical and psychological maladies in our modern age than any other time in history,[2,3] despite being in a world with more answers than ever before. As our species evolved to survive unfamiliar environments, our brains learned to perceive anything we didn't understand as a potential threat until proven otherwise.[4] This approach helped us to survive in our migratory ancestry, but today our fear of the unknown leaves us in a constant state of stress.

We have an overwhelming desire to decide our plans for the future now, because we're uncomfortable remaining in limbo. Instead of embracing a feeling of uncertainty as an opportunity to tap into our authentic desires, we prematurely force the open cycles of life closed.

The Brain Thinks in Beginnings and Endings

Often the clashes between our conscious and subconscious attractions exist because our dislike of uncertainty leads us to prematurely seek endings. We like to perceive the world in terms of beginnings and endings, or cycles. We rarely tell a friend a story without an ending, even if the ending is only "And now I'm here." We favor films and TV series with conclusive endings. And sports matches that end in a tie are dissatisfying compared to games with a definitive winner. We want to follow a concept, goal, or storyline from beginning to tidy ending. When we reach the end of a cycle, we can pack it in a box and shove it in the attic and not have to think about it anymore.

When a cycle is open, incomplete, or lacking a definite conclusion, we often feel anxiety until we achieve closure. It's like a song ending on a seventh instead of the key chord—we feel on edge, waiting for the harmonic resolve. It's why most people hate the ending of *Lost*, a six-season mystery/thriller. The promise of every story is an ending, so ones that end in more questions can cause disparaging reviews. The final episode was unsatisfying because it left the audience with more questions than answers. Open cycles are extremely frustrating.

If we're having trouble closing a cycle, we make up an ending to quell our anxiety—even if our manufactured resolution is artificial, inaccurate, or otherwise insufficient. When we are midway through our cycle and stop making progress, we seek premature closure, and we'll even be willing to believe a lie if it means we can feel a sense of certainty again. We create forced endings because we are too impatient to allow the full cycle to take place.

While seeking premature closure of our cycles, we are often motivated by two driving impulses: 1) to find closure quickly, and 2) to close the cycle forever. In psychology, these motivations for closure are known as the urgency tendency and permanence tendency.[5]

The expediency and finality of these impulses can drive wild miscalculations and misinterpretations about ourselves and the world around us. We jump to the conclusion that our colleague hates us because we can't stand not knowing if she will walk into the office each morning grumpy or happy. Best to just assume she doesn't like us and keep our distance, we may think. We might see a friend who isn't sure whether his partner is "the one" give the partner an ultimatum to propose or break up after a year of dating in order to force a false permanent solution.

To better understand how we came to prefer false solutions over waiting for a natural end to the cycle, it helps to learn our evolutionary history and its challenges in the modern world.

There were always clear solutions for simple problems. If there wasn't enough food, we would hunt or farm for more. If there wasn't a warm place to stay out of the rain, we would erect shelters from palm fronds, animal hides, and wooden beams. If we feared a midnight marauding from wolves, we'd build perimeter defenses, organize a night guard, or sleep in a cliffside inaccessible to our four-legged foes.

For most of our time on earth, humankind's primary focus was to resolve these simple cycles, but today, a majority of people in industrialized nations are instead faced with complex cycles. We are plagued with questions of how to find love, how to garner respect, and how to fulfill our life's purpose. These cycles are not as easy to close as finding some berries to eat. Yet, we possess an impulse to address these open cycles with an expedient response. Today, the absence of connection, status, or freedom might feel as stressful to a sales representative as hunting down a wild pig felt to our prehistoric ancestors.

With less tangible and less attainable desires, we are enmeshed in an endless state of open-cycle anxiety. Every day we face a choice: take control of our own destiny and bring our cycle to a rough-hewn end, or be crushed under the weight of our own neuroses. Many of us choose to force our cycles closed with false answers rather than face our anxiety. The false security of a hastily closed cycle often feels better than jumping into the unknown to examine our subconscious attractions.

The desire to close our cycles is evident in the case of the most decorated gymnast in history, Simone Biles.[6] In 2021 she suffered a debilitating breakdown, which impaired her ability to compete in the Olympics. Biles had devoted her life to perfecting her craft, foregoing typical teenage activities for the honor of being America's Athletic

Sweetheart. Her Mercury Mind approved as she was pushed to her limits by her family, her team, and the American public.

In the midst of her dogged pursuit, she was molested by longtime national team doctor Lawrence Nassar. In interviews and testimonies about Nassar, Simone describes how she minimized the abuse's impact. At the time, dismissing the abuse allowed her to convince herself the cycle was closed so she could pursue her conscious goal of making athletic history. She told herself that becoming the world's most famous and awarded gymnast would make her happy, but that solution only satisfied her for a few years.

In the end, Simone Biles was miserable because her authentic desire was not to be the most famous gymnast in U.S. history. In the core of her heart, she wanted to be cared for and loved for being who she was, not for what she could do.

Biles had a difficult childhood.[7] Her mother was addicted to drugs and alcohol and Simone was often hungry and neglected. She recounted that her mother fed the household cat before her and her siblings. After being taken into child protective services and passed around the foster care system, Simone was eventually adopted by her maternal grandparents at age six. Her search for love didn't end there, however. Her grandmother admitted it took time to bond with Simone and her sister because the children had been severely traumatized.

Simone's grandmother eventually connected with the girls but, by then, Simone had already committed to a conscious plan of finding love and belonging through gymnastics.[8]

While achieving incredible success as an athlete allowed Simone to close her cycles, the activity was riddled with toxicity. Her historic Olympic status meant the public cared about her as an athlete, but, deep down, she wanted someone to care about her as a person. The ad nauseam dismissal of her mental health and physical wellbeing by her Olympic team and sponsors made her feel unimportant, even while the media hailed her as one of the most important athletes of her time. The disregard for her authentic desires was compounded by the abuse of Dr. Nassar. Instead of discovering healthier ways to close her open cycle of craving belonging and self-worth, Simone stuck with conscious attraction to athletic prowess for years, leading to mental and physical distress. Her superficial solution usurped her joy of achieving international athletic recognition. Her depression, anxiety, and the ankle 'twisties,' could not be alleviated until she reopened her cycle and faced her deeper attractions towards acceptance and self-respect.

Fortunately, Simone's tale has a happy, open ending. Biles came forward with her abuse testimony in 2021 and joined the community advocating for mental health improvement in her sport. She made the courageous decision to re-open her closed cycle and continue on a healthy path toward true care and belonging. After re-opening the loop, she received attention and support from her fans, and with her Mercury Mind freed from toxic conscious desires she began a journey toward her authentic desire for loving affection. In 2021, Time Magazine named Simone Biles Athlete of the Year.[9] They awarded her recognition not because of her athleticism, but because of her humanity.

Like Simone Biles, when we prematurely force closure of our cycles we can evoke anxiety, depression, and anger. These feelings continue until we are able to face the deeper desire behind the cycle. In order to find a pathway to true closure, we must recognize and accept there is an unmet, deeper, lingering attraction. We must re-open the cycle to allow ourselves to continue along the journey.

When we force our cycles closed, we suppress our authentic desires in favor of a certain ending. Doing this keeps our Mercury Mind in a toxic state as we cling to our new conscious desire. We often become addicted to the conscious desires we use to prematurely close our cycles.

Becoming Addicted to Conscious Desires

When we force a cycle closed, we may succeed in relieving our anxiety temporarily. We can artificially stave off uncertainty and experience a high. This feeling is usually coupled with increased levels of self-confidence. We think, yes! We made it to the end, we completed a goal.

Now we can rest in the confidence that we can handle anything that comes our way by simply closing a cycle.

Like any addiction, we become dependent on the temporary relief of false certainty and we then seek to close ever more cycles to assuage our discomfort over the unpredictability of life. Of course, the temporary salve of forcing our cycles shut is not a sustainable strategy because it does not relieve the subconscious drive to realize our authentic attractions.

Our dependency on conscious desires occurs from an early age, when we are taught to suppress, divert, and compromise our subconscious desires. We are often made to feel ashamed of our true wants. The exact messages vary depending on the environment—for example, growing up with parents who are hippies is different from growing up with lawyers—but the outcome is the same. As we mature, we are restricted by social and cultural mores and suppress our authentic selves to better fit in. We meld our Mercury Mind to match others' expectations. We learn people want us to be a specific way, and so we change ourselves to fit in.

But shifting our identity to achieve a conscious plan of fitting in with a social group will only create toxic Mercury Mind connections. True Mercury Mind connections exist only when we freely pursue our authentic desires. Melding ourselves in an effort to connect with others results in toxic, volatile bonds. We can see this play out in teenagers all the time.

Teens are still figuring out who they are and so they might try out different social groups to see what they like best. This sampling process leads to constant drama. To fit in with different social circles teens are compelled to change parts of themselves. The young people that avoid drama are those who find social groups and activities that are more aligned with their authentic attractions.

We try to mold ourselves to be what we think others want, but this practice is toxic.

When we are rejected for expressing our authentic selves we internalize a sense of shame. We learn to hide our desires, even from ourselves. We may stop admitting even to ourselves what we really want out of fear we'll be rejected. To ease these burgeoning feelings of shame, we cope through committing a socially-acceptable conscious plan. We tell ourselves we really want to score an A in Math, try out for the basketball team, and get into a brand-name college, even if these things don't truly appeal to us. Pursuing false conscious goals is a way of forcing our cycles closed. Instead of giving ourselves space to explore our options and see what feels best, we jump to the next logical conscious plan. And so the cycle repeats.

Over time, we become experts at closing cycles with conscious plans. Eventually, we succeed in convincing ourselves that our false, socially-approved goals are more real than what lies underneath. As we bend and mold ourselves to gain acceptance our Mercury Mind enters a toxic state.

Dennis Rader, also known as the Blind-Torture-Kill (BTK) Killer, is an extreme example of this toxic Mercury Mind dynamic. A family man, boy scout leader, and member of the church council, he gruesomely murdered ten people between 1974 and 1991.[10] While his public persona was socially acceptable, his private, homicidal tendencies were clearly an expression of his repressed subconscious attractions. He seems to have killed to satisfy his desire for acknowledgement. He publicly and regularly taunted the police, seeming to enjoy the attention he received, and in one infamous correspondence, he asked, *"How many do I have to kill before I get a name in the paper or some national recognition?"*

Underneath Dennis Rader's fetish was a man who desperately wanted to be famous. Deep down, Dennis Rader resented his parents for neglecting him in his childhood[11]. It seems his original subconscious desire to be accepted, recognized, and loved by his caretakers was grossly perverted by multiple layers of distorted coping mechanisms.

Fortunately, most of us don't twist our desires to such an unhealthy degree as Dennis Rader, but many of us do become addicted to escalating conscious plans. We indulge our conscious desires over our more authentic wants because we are addicted to closing our cycles.

Fulfilling our small conscious desires and gaining approval from others gives us dopamine hits, but this pattern is unsustainable. We might receive a high from being seen as worthy by others for our accomplishments, possessions, or appearance. But by repressing our true desires to fit in we are viewing our authentic selves as unworthy. This ultimately destroys our self-esteem. The more we shift away from ourselves, the more toxicity permeates our Mercury Mind.

Humans loathe uncertainty because the unknown could spell danger, and this fear of the unknown extends not simply to new environments, but also to our own minds. We try to control this overwhelming fear by staking claim to what we do know. From classic literature to contemporary YouTube videos, we've been taught that at the very least we should be able to know ourselves. When we think we do not understand an aspect of our own psyche, the impulse is often to neutralize the unknown parts of ourselves we see as threats. We make a conscious plan, close the cycle, and move on.

Even those of us who have done extensive self-work are susceptible to grasping for answers we can use to force our cycles closed. A nervous man may diagnose himself with an anxiety disorder through a quiz on the back of a magazine. A wanderlusting woman might listen to the psychic who foresees a better career opportunity for her if she picks up everything and moves cities. A woman who resents her parents may find a therapist who tells her she can't maintain a romantic relationship because of her unresolved issues with her father.

When we take on false conscious plans for what we want in our lives we also search for answers as to why we don't have those things yet. This is another way of helping us avoid the uncertainty within. With so many external sources of reassurance at our disposal like supportive friends, self-help doctrines, and therapists who tell us what we want to hear, it is no wonder we are more apt to look outside than inside for answers. This persistent distraction keeps the cork of our subconscious desires frozen solid, and leads to loneliness, depression, and perceived victimhood. We believe the unknown elements within ourselves are foreign and unnatural, but these aspects of our psyche may actually be the most natural parts of who we are. Just because we don't fully understand something doesn't mean we can't embrace it.

Feelings like dissatisfaction, loneliness, depression, anger, and anxiety are all signals that our subconscious desires need attention. If we don't check in with our authentic attractions by recognizing they exist, we might drive ourselves to commit unhealthy behaviors. But it can be difficult to acknowledge our true desires because we tend to double-down on our conscious beliefs when faced with uncertainty.

When We Get It Wrong, We Double-Down

Instead of acknowledging our deep-seated dissatisfaction with our poorly-closed cycles, we cling to the medications that give us a temporary feeling of satisfaction. We obsess over our highs because, if we didn't, we would have to acknowledge our problematic approaches. We would have to do the difficult work of sitting with our uncertainty as a cycle slowly progresses from beginning to ending, which is often too uncomfortable. Instead of prying open our hastily closed cycles like Simone did, we reinforce them.

Playing off our misshapen cycles is like a gambling addict who continues to frequent the high-stakes poker table on weekends. Most of the time, he loses. On the occasional trip to the casino, he wins big. Nonetheless, these rare wins can't outweigh the losses. He's almost always in the red, yet he fixates on the week or two he's in the black. He remembers the Royal Flush and four-ace hand last month, but not the three-week streak of losing it all on fool-hardy bluffs. If he consciously recalled his losses, he would consequently acknowledge his debts and recognize his toxic behavior of borrowing money. He would stop doubling down on winning at cards and instead examine what he really wants. What deeper desire is driving his conscious plan of hitting the jackpot? Maybe he craves financial security or an adrenaline rush.

It is often easier to weather the pains of a hastily closed cycle than face the long pathway toward an uncertain ending. With time, our small pains build on each other until we are hunched under a heavy weight of our own making. Deep down, we know we're the victim of our own habits, but we cling to our false answers like a life raft. The longer we stay in denial, the more we poison our Mercury Minds with toxic vaporous compounds.

To make up for our feelings of inadequacy, we often seek confirmation that we are worthy. We do things we know others will approve of so we can gain validation. Maybe we buy a new motorcycle and go show it off at a biker bar because we know people there will be impressed. In psychology, this is known as confirmation bias.[12] When we reinforce our shoddily closed cycles by seeking out people who will validate our conscious plans, we are doubling down on inauthenticity.

The Pizzagate conspiracy theorists are a perfect example of this tendency to seek validation of our conscious plans from people who we know will approve. Between 2016 and 2020, allegations that Democratic leaders were abusing children ballooned into a massive following under the name QAnon. This group was largely responsible for the capitol riot on January 6, 2021.[13] QAnon grew out of frustrations with the social, political, and economic environment bred from the Trump presidency and the COVID-19 pandemic, and became an umbrella coalition for a host of conspiracy theories from federal Satanism to the faked suicide of Jeffery Epstein.[14]

In its most basic incarnation, QAnon collected people with fears of the unknown. Its rise was predicated by an atypical administration, a worldwide pandemic, and a flailing economy. Widespread uncertainty led to mass panic and a desperate scramble to explain the unknown. As is often the case with conspiracy theories, the people most susceptible to indoctrination were more likely to report mental health diagnoses.[15] In other words, people who struggled with difficult emotions and low self-esteem were susceptible to wide-scale manipulation.

When QAnon prophecies failed to materialize, such as the date of Trump retaking office after losing the 2020 election, believers held to their convictions more than ever. No amount of counter evidence could prove to them their theories were unbased. On the contrary, their beliefs became more outlandish as far-fetched concepts are harder to disprove. The story morphed to include elaborate cover-up tactics used by the Clintons to hide the ritualistic child sacrifice occurring in the basement of a pizza shop. Except, that pizza shop actually has no basement.

Holding strong to ridiculous beliefs and failing to acknowledge counter evidence promotes an "us versus them" mentality. This black-

and-white view is often rooted in hastily closed cycles. Rather than facing the discomfort of acknowledging messy theories, we cling to perspectives that subvert ambiguity and protect our fragile egos. When presented with information that challenges or dismantles our closures, we give more weight to people who align with our pre-existing conscious views, even if they are less reliable.[16]

The consequence of doubling down on our false sense of closure is that we often drift farther from meeting our true desires. The only way to combat this trajectory is to allow ourselves to sit in uncertainty and let our cycles lead us to a natural ending.

Walking the Uncertain Path

At the end of the 1967 film *The Graduate*, the protagonist Ben bangs on the glass-panels of the church balcony overlooking the wedding of his ex-girlfriend.[17] "Elaine!" he screams. "Elaainnne!"

In her white dress and bridal veil, Elaine breaks her kiss with the country club Ken doll she was about to marry and rushes toward her ex, shouting "Ben!"

The church's stunned silence breaks into chaos as Ben runs down the stairs to grab Elaine. In a markedly sacrilegious moment, Ben fends off well-wishers with a large wooden cross and seals them in the church. He and Elaine run and hop onto the Santa Barbara Municipal bus the second it pulls away from the station. Disheveled, elated, and unfazed by the glares of the other bus passengers, they share a moment of ecstatic freedom.

This would be the perfect happy ending, but the camera doesn't cut away. Instead, it captures Ben and Elaine turning away from each other. Their expressions shift from ecstasy to existential dread as they realize the magnitude of their decision. They've gotten what they want, and they're not happy. They nervously ponder what comes next.

The film version of *The Graduate* is not a love story. It is a story about our relationship with uncertainty. In the beginning of the movie, Ben attends his college graduation party and struggles while family friends bombard him with the infernal question, "What are you going to do now?" After all of his awards and accolades, Ben believes he should have an answer and he doesn't. He should be able to produce a profound response to allay that one guest's mundane solution of 'plastics.' Ben runs to his room to dodge the identity crisis.

Ben's struggle with his uncertainty leaves him vulnerable, so he copes by pursuing love with Mrs. Robinson. When he exhausts his trysts with Mrs. Robinson, he distracts himself again through a tumultuous affair with Elaine. In the final bus scene, Ben's deflection attempt crumbles to the apt anthem of Simon & Garfunkel's *The Sound of Silence*. Now that he's gotten what he told himself he wanted Ben must finally face his own uncertainty head on, and it terrifies him.

Ben seeks to assuage his unease about what he wants through intimacy. He believes a relationship could resolve his unknown future. When he realizes it won't work with Mrs. Robinson, he doubles-down in his pursuit of intimacy through his relationship with Elaine. When he realizes Elaine won't fix his deep-rooted feelings of uncertainty about his future, he ends up in the same crumby position where he started.

The Graduate stands the test of time because it doesn't pander to our desire for closure, Hollywood endings, or tying up loose ends. Viewers hope for a completed cycle. We expect to watch Ben move from longing, to chasing, to fulfilling his deepest desires. Then we want him to live happily ever after. Except, he doesn't. Instead, Ben has the uncomfortable realization that he'd been trying to force his cycle closed by pursuing the conscious goal of winning Elaine's love. The moment on the bus is so powerful because it shows Ben and Elaine realizing they must re-open their cycles.

When we become comfortable with uncertainty, we're less apt to close cycles too quickly. When we can sit with uncertainty, we can stave off the noxious gasses from our Mercury Minds and reunite with our most authentic selves.

At the end of *The Graduate*, Elaine and Ben finally run away together and display elation as Ben throws his head back with a laugh and Elaine meets his gaze with a look of unbridled triumph. Yet, this moment of jubilation is impaled by the dagger of deeper unmet attractions, uncertainty about the future, and disregard for a healthy path forward.

Like the expressions slowly shifting on Ben and Elaine's faces at the end of *The Graduate*, dissatisfaction and anxiety slowly creep in once we realize chasing conscious plans can no longer distract us from our true attractions. We all go through similar moments every time we realize we've been pursuing a relationship that satisfies our conscious plans rather than our authentic desires.

If Ben from *The Graduate* had let himself be uncomfortable, he may have recognized his need to prove himself and searched for a healthy way to do that. He could have kept his cycle open instead of jumping so quick into the pursuit of dead-end relationships. He may have been able to let himself soak in his own discomfort until five, ten, or fifteen years later when a fulfilling opportunity came to him. And at that point, he could pursue a healthier relationship with others. Then he would finally feel self-esteem and belonging. From that place of authenticity he would be able to connect more deeply with others.

The challenge with sitting in our uncertainty is that it's aggravating. The unknown exposes incompleteness. To accept the uncertain is to be vulnerable, which is difficult without high self-esteem. For most of us, low self-esteem is partially responsible for our desire to expediently close our cycles. In other words, we are insecure about our authenticity, and so we supplement shoddy endings to our cycles instead of waiting for a natural conclusion. Herein lies the catch-22. We must become comfortable with uncertainty to build our self-esteem, but in order to be comfortable with uncertainty, high self-esteem helps.

The antidote to this conundrum is awareness. Recognizing uncertainty exists is the first step to accepting it. It is perfectly natural and healthy to have open cycles. These are common and temporary. Some cycles may begin and end quickly, while others may last decades. Know that every cycle will end, but to force them closed early is unhealthy. In the interim, we must be patient with ourselves and know that our vulnerability in the midst of an open cycle is inexorably human.

Recognize we can neither seek nor force closure. When we allow cycles to take their natural course, we can observe ourselves. With unclosed cycles, we can notice our subconscious attractions and how we are drawn to them, even if we are unable to explain them. Through this allowance, we give ourselves room to better identify ourselves. And we must know ourselves before we can become comfortable with ourselves.

We will learn to develop self-esteem and self-confidence without artificially pursuing it through promotions, material objects, or sexual fantasies. With more self-esteem we can tap into our true selves without being afraid. We can accept ourselves through understanding our strengths and weaknesses with openness and this helps us be more authentic with the rest of the world. Without fear of the uncertain, we can sit with ourselves and better comprehend our deepest attractions without the need for sudden, artificial closure.

However, this entire process is not easy in the short term. It is uncomfortable at first as it will conjure some inner demons and bring us face-to-face with parts of ourselves formerly kept under lock and key. Wonderfully, the end of our journey will present true closure. We will find connection. We will find authenticity. We will be truly satisfied.

When we adopt a conscious attraction so we can force a cycle closed, we ignore the deeper attractions within. With forced closure, our authentic self is dissatisfied because our true desires remain unmet. Despite accolades, achievements, or acclaim, we feel a lingering sense of disquietude if our true attractions are not brought to fruition. Underneath all the praise, we sense our falsely closed cycle is about to bust open.

This is why so many rock stars overdose on heroin, happily married CEOs have marital affairs, and champion football players get arrested for drunk driving. Each of these individuals may have a high level of confidence from repeatedly forcing their cycles closed, but they know something still isn't right. They haven't yet realized their authentic attractions and their Mercury Mind has turned toxic as they try to meld themselves into what someone else wants. They need to re-open the cycle and examine it more closely. But this involves facing the uncertainty of achieving our genuine desires.

3

Self-Confidence Trap

Most self-help strategies promote confidence as an important piece of achieving your goals and finding fulfillment.

"Self-confidence is the first requisite to great undertakings," wrote Samuel Johnson.

"It is confidence in our bodies, minds, and spirits that allow us to keep looking for new adventures," proffered Oprah Winfrey.

"The most beautiful thing you can wear is confidence," said Blake Lively.

But confidence only gets us so far. If we are confident in our adventuring skills and know nothing about the road ahead, we might march directly into the maw of danger. If we are confident in our ability to lead a nation without doing the research to understand its people, we might end up with our head on a spike. If we show up for a date highly confident in our accomplishments, we might attract only gold-digging partners.

Many self-improvement methods focus on accomplishing goals as a way to build self-confidence. These philosophies usually promote a "fake it 'til you make it" attitude in which we should posture confidence until we feel it. However, this is exactly the sort of behavior that furthers the suppression of authentic attractions.

The popular self-help advice can work. Achieving goals can certainly make us feel more confident, especially if we choose goals we know others will approve of. However, the issue with a confidence-centric approach is that it makes us feel assured in the face of uncertainty. Confidence feeds into our addiction to prematurely closing our cycles and gives us a temporary high in the face of the unknown.

The popular self-help technique of power posing demonstrates many of the issues with confidence. A power pose is a way of standing that makes people automatically *feel* more confident. We are told that if we can master the art of puffing out our chests and standing up straight, we will be able to land a corporate executive position. But confidence is a temporary way to cover up a lack of self-esteem. By focusing on confidence we neglect looking into why we are so stressed out about the big job interview to begin with.

Our well-meaning friends and mentors might shout things like, "You can do this!," "You're so great!," or "You can be anything you want to be!," and these lines can pump us full of quick-fix confidence. But these platitudes are not a permanent remedy for our uneasy feelings. A pump-up speech is not going to teach us how to pass the medical exam, how to run for office, or how to demonstrate to our employer we're ready to take on more responsibility. It also does not allow us to look inside ourselves for answers about what we want.

Not all self-help books are so blatant in their worship of confidence, but the undercurrent runs through many of the best selling titles in the genre. The grandfather of self-help books, *How to Win Friends and Influence People*[1] has a seven-principle guideline for making connections. These principles include advice such as "praise is more effective than criticism," "encourage others to talk, and listen carefully when they do," and "get others to agree with you from the start, and then gently lead them to your conclusions." Each of these concepts is aimed at building the skill of communication. According to author Dale Carnegie, if you learn to compliment others, give them the floor, or promote your point of view to them, you will create strong relationships.

Each of these Carnegie-recommended skills builds our confidence in our ability to win friends and connect with others.

However, as soon as we encounter an obstacle that these strategies can't handle, our confidence plummets and our relationships begin to disintegrate. We meet a person who perceives our compliments as inauthentic, and our confidence dips ten points. We go on a date with someone who wants to hear about us rather than talk incessantly about themselves, and the harder we try to show a sincere interest in them the more they pull away. We give an enticing presentation at work and our boss demolishes our proposed project with his feedback. Our confidence plummets when our strategies don't work.

Self-confidence is a feeling we build by developing an aptitude for something. We can have confidence we are a strong swimmer, a loyal friend, or attractive mate. These are abilities that can fluctuate with changes in our relationships, environment, and health. When our skills are put to the test beyond our measure, our confidence wanes. The person who has confidence in their swimming abilities might feel worthless when they get cut from the swim team. The woman who prides herself on her friendliness might have a breakdown when she finds out an acquaintance perceived her as rude. The guy who keeps his physique trim and his shirts ironed might cry into a double shot of whiskey when the hottest girl in the room chooses the tubby guy with a great sense of humor instead of him. When confidence decreases, we are once again left in a position of uncertainty as our cycles burst open.

Building self-confidence relates to achieving our conscious attractions, not necessarily our authentic subconscious desires. Whenever our ability to achieve our conscious attractions shifts, so does our confidence. This means our confidence is in constant flux based on external stimuli. When we rely on confidence as a measure of ourselves, our identity becomes a reflection of our skillfulness at something and our abilities become the reason we are valuable and deserving of love and belonging.

This is what happened to Simone Biles. She was incredibly self-confident in her gymnastic ability, but that self-confidence didn't leave her fulfilled. This is sadly common in high achievers. Problems arise when these top performers struggle to achieve ever greater success.

People often feel inadequate and slip into major depressive episodes when they tie their self-worth to their ability to perform.

Confidence-first methodologies place the emphasis on fulfilling our conscious desires. But these teachings presume we already know what we want. While conscious desires can be a superficial reflection of subconscious attractions, this is not always the case. In fact, sometimes our conscious desires can lead us farther away from our authentic desires.

Self-help dogma often fails to help us explore, understand, and accept our internal worlds. Popular psychology books and videos emphasize strengthening our ability to mitigate our external world, which is such a monumental task that it distracts us from getting in touch with ourselves. Raising our level of self-confidence is a temporary solution, because, like forcing a cycle closed, it dismisses the importance of our inner authentic self in favor of external success. This naturally creates a toxic environment for our Mercury Minds.

Confidence is commonly mistaken for self-esteem because both make us feel better about ourselves. Self-confidence assures us of our skillfulness, whereas self-esteem is a feeling that we are deeply worthy as people. The former requires proof of our merits, which shows the world we are good. The latter requires internal work, and believing to *ourselves* that even though we're flawed we're still ok. The difference between confidence and self-esteem is the distinction between saying, "I am good at something" and "I am good."

While confidence requires constant reaffirmation, self-esteem is self-affirming. Self-esteem is infinite in its energy and capacity to fuel us, so long as we do not forcibly stop it. It's like the difference between a regular machine, which requires gas to function, and a perpetual motion machine, which doesn't need any additional fuel to sustain itself. Both confidence and self-esteem can sustain us, but only one can do so long-term.

When we address our self-esteem, we are better able to see ourselves as we are and connect with our subconscious desires. This is the basis to forming authentic relationships with other people. We don't need to understand or know everything about ourselves to have self-esteem, we simply need to fully accept the person we are. Self-esteem lets us feel comfortable with keeping our cycles open for as long as they need to be open without rushing to close them.

There is a huge focus on confidence in our culture. And confidence certainly isn't bad. But it's a distraction. It won't help us build deeper relationships like self-esteem will.

Confidence Is Not the Answer

"When you don't text a girl back, that's the most powerful message you can send," says David de las Morenas in one of his videos.[2] David runs a million-subscriber YouTube Channel called *How to Beast*, which aims to help men build confidence (and muscles). His videos are a compilation of dating and life advice punctuated by weightlifting montages and shots of his girlfriend's backside. In this video, David describes the rules for texting women.

If a woman dares to waffle on meeting time or suggest meeting in a group instead of one-on-one, David advocates for using negligence to induce feelings of guilt, shame, and a desperate need to rectify the situation.

"Yeah," David's girlfriend echoes in the video. "You have to put her in her place."

David offers other hard-set rules during this texting masterclass, including:

- If she takes thirty minutes to respond, make sure you take thirty minutes to respond.
- If she sends a short text, send a short text in return.
- Don't send more than one text in a row.
- If she wants to take more time to get to know you through texting, respond with a cute little put-down, "That's the point of the date, silly!"

David's approach takes the uncertainty out of dating by giving his followers a set of simple rules to follow. He claims there are certain triggers that lead to specific outcomes, and so we can open and close cycles by leveraging those patterns. This approach boxes out the uncertainty of dating and provides temporary relief to guys hesitant in the dating sphere. David believes men can get women to chase them if the men decide to leave the women hanging on unsatisfactory text messages. Essentially, he is teaching us how to keep the cycle with women open so they will feel the need to close it.

The problem with David's approach is that it sometimes is successful and then builds confidence in those for whom it works.

"Bruh this has worked for so long," states one user in the comments section of the video. "When the girls play you, you play them back immediately. They love that shit lol."

These texting games do entice women to respond, often because they are confused. It's easy to understand how a vague text might prompt an innocent recipient to ask for clarification.

The issue with committing to rigid rules of behavior is that it removes the chances of finding an authentic connection. Having rules about people means, over time, we become more focused on the rules and the game of interacting instead of looking to connect authentically with the other person in the exchange. Playing cat-and-mouse can be exhilarating, but when the cat catches the mouse, the game is over. The man who lands a date with a hard-to-get woman faces a new challenge: continue to win her affection through carefully-selected scripts, or revert to the organic conversations that failed to land him a date in the first place. If the man who plays cat values the woman's affection over acting his authentic self, he will likely choose the former. Similarly, if we use tricks, tactics and sets of rules to win over a boss, colleague, potential friend, or family member, we deny ourselves the opportunity to deeply connect and find the meaningful relationships that make our lives richer.

The interactions David's followers might have can never lead to finding a true Mercury Mind connection because by nature of following a strict set of rules, the men (or women) who subscribe to them will view others as prizes to be won. His channel is about how to win women, not create fulfilling relationships.

David's process inspires feelings of confidence, control, and cunning in those who use it, but the approach is not a roadmap for building true connections. His guidelines for texting rely on a universal script that leaves little wiggle-room to respond with personality, authenticity, or honesty. He's calling on us to suppress our Mercury Mind attractions and use rigid strategies to enter into relationships with people who we might not even like, but who are recognized by wider society as good matches for us. If a person isn't naturally drawn to us, chances are nothing we can say aloud or in a text message will make them feel a deep and enduring attraction. If we adopt an alternate personality to attract a certain person, we will have to make a conscious effort to suppress our true selves. Eventually we will always reveal our true colors. Any interpersonal gains from David's process are temporary because the relationship isn't built on a bedrock of authenticity, it is constructed on a paper-thin foundation of fleeting confidence.

Like *How to Beast*, many of the tactics found in self-help books are built on our desire to eliminate uncomfortable feelings of uncertainty. If we can predict how a woman will react when we text her in a specific way, then the uncertainty disappears and we've closed the cycle. If we find some success we will gain confidence, which assuages our discomfort over dating in the first place.

This by-the-book approach operates under the flawed assumption that all people will respond similarly and want the same things. In truth, David's method works on a small subsection of the female populace. Why focus on such a small group just to build confidence that will crumble when an interaction doesn't go according to plan?

When we presume all people will respond in a universal way, we discount the differences between various human beings. For example, a 2010 study found Indian women preferred to text when they were alone, as they received negative reactions when they texted in others' proximity.[3] This was not true of U.S. women, who rarely reported such criticism for texting in company. If a woman of Indian cultural heritage fails to respond in a timely manner, it may be more an indication of her surrounding company than her level of interest in a suitor. If a man reacts to a delayed text by peevishly punishing her, she may be confused or frustrated at his lack of understanding. These feelings of dejection might encourage her to put more effort into winning the man's affection, leading to a doomed relationship of subordination.

Or, she might decide to invest in a person who better understands her behaviors and won't act churlish when she's being authentic. Either way, David's texting rules would fail in this situation.

Further, common sense tells us not all women want the same thing. On a superficial level, one woman might want to be a career-first chemical engineer, another might want to be a stay-at-home mother, and a third might want to be a lesbian who builds houses for *Habitat for Humanity*. These three women probably want different types of relationships with a man: a supporter, a provider, or a friend.

When we homogenize people through a set script, we ignore the Mercury Mind's natural attraction to compatible individuals and we huff the toxic fumes of Mercury vapor instead. Imagine the Mercury Mind like a cosmic force beyond our control. When someone is attracted to us, they are naturally drawn toward us just as mercury is naturally attracted to itself.

If the chemistry is not there, it never will be. Mixing mercury with pure water leads to a null interaction as the two liquids can coexist without any reactivity. You can put them in a blender and get them to mix temporarily, but it doesn't last. Similarly, even if someone is fooled by a script at first, nature will win out in the end. The speaker will either revert to their true self after maintaining an exhausting facade, or the mouse will find the cat to be nothing more than a stuffed toy. If your scripts do attract someone to bind with your Mercury Mind, an unhealthy interaction will occur. The Mercury Mind will produce toxic compounds and poison both parties.

Rigid Rules Suppress Mercury Mind Connections

Even if our adherence to rules does attract a healthy match and we are lucky enough to stumble into a Mercury Mind connection, the techniques prevent us from being authentic. When we look up quick-fix pick-up lines, we might reduce the uncertainty of making an authentic connection with the person who strikes our fancy. We're trying to force the cycle to an abrupt end through temporary, scripted confidence, which prevents us from making contact rooted in authenticity. The tendency to rely on quick fixes rather than being vulnerable suggests an unsustainable future. If we aren't comfortable being vulnerable in relationships, we are likely to experience disconnection at some point down the line.

To illustrate this point, let's see how David de las Morenas' advice applies to the long term. Imagine the stars align and a woman responds exactly as David predicts. An insecure guy named Ricky wins over a supermodel girlfriend named Shayla and they continue following the rules for a few weeks. After a month of following the rules and receiving the predicted outcomes, Ricky doesn't respond to one of Shayla's texts because the day prior she canceled plans at the last minute to babysit her niece. Shayla apologizes to Ricky profusely until he responds. Ricky resents Shayla's priorities and Shayla starts to question Ricky's lack of compassion.

Six months later, Shayla asks Ricky, "How do you feel about it?" when Ricky unexpectedly loses his job.

He responds, "I'm ok," abiding by the shorter-the-better principle. Ricky wants to express more, but doesn't want to deviate from the script that got him the hot girlfriend. Shayla aches to connect with Ricky, but increasingly feels Ricky is unapproachable. She wonders if there's anything going on below the surface of what Ricky presents to her.

Fast-forward six months and Shayla asks Ricky to pick the dog up from the vet. She hadn't responded to Ricky's previous text, "Babe, I'm going out for beers with the guys tonight," for forty-five minutes.

Ricky, abiding by David's advice, waits forty-five minutes to respond. By that time, Shayla has canceled an important interview and is pulling up outside the vet. The two engage in a no-holds-barred argument when she arrives home, leading to their eventual break-up. While most people are wise enough not to take pick-up strategies to the extreme like Ricky, this example shows how scripts can corrode a relationship.

There is no universally right answer for the way we should connect with people. If others want to connect with us, they will.

Even if a particular script aids us in making an initial connection, it is true authenticity that will sustain the relationship. Without authenticity, even a relationship founded in a genuine Mercury Mind connection can deteriorate. The more Ricky clings to his one-size-fits-all rules, the longer he delays making a genuine connection with Shayla. He values manipulations to eliminate uncertainty over the difficult yet rewarding work of connecting with another human being. This leads to an ultimately fatal attraction and a bitter breakup. The lesson is clear: we can script a transaction, but we cannot script a relationship.

Rules play on our desire for confidence. They neutralize feelings of uncertainty while creating a false pretense. Most people who are drawn to self-help teachings like David's are deeply uncomfortable with truly connecting. They are uncertain about their relationships and this leads them to grasp at manipulations. They scramble to close their cycles, but in the process cut off the path to true intimacy. They create a hollow doppelganger of themselves to act out their relationships without acknowledging their true attractions. This fake persona has a short shelf-life, as does any relationship predicated on it. At first, Ricky may feel confident in his relationship because the script works, but in the end he sacrifices genuine connection for self-confidence. Ironically, the confidence he works so hard to maintain is shattered when the couple breaks up.

We cannot truly connect with real people unless we are authentic and comfortable in our own skin. When we use disingenuous tactics to win someone over, the relationship is based on a fake connection. While this can work out for a short-term, transactional relationship, any long-term relationship requires more substance to grow and flourish.

Illusions of Self-Esteem

Self-confidence can masquerade as self-esteem, so it's critical we don't confuse them. The use of scripts is a classic self-esteem mimic. When we approach our relationships with a quick-fix script, we can appear to have all the self-esteem in the world. However, scripts are fragile and cannot lay a blueprint for an entire relationship, so we should avoid them. We might think we don't use scripts, but many of us have go-to phrases we use to defuse tensions in our close relationships.

For example, if our partner is upset with a mistake we made, we might default to the classic script, "You're right. I'm wrong. I'm sorry I didn't listen to you. I'm going to do a better job of listening to you from now on. Can you forgive me for being such an idiot?"

The wonderful quality of this script is its flexibility. In many arguments this script can cool down an angry partner and get them to level with you. The rub is it is disingenuous. When we apply the same conflict-avoidant dialogue to every fight, we stop listening to our partners. We deliver the lines we know will be a get-out-of-jail-free card without taking the more arduous, uncomfortable, self-reflective approach of uncovering why the argument arose and how we can work through it. We need self-esteem to be honest and discern our role in a fight, but with just a bit of self-confidence we can repeat the magic words and temporarily dodge discomfort. Instead of relying on self-confidence to mitigate our fights without listening, we should leverage self-esteem to acknowledge our faults without shame. The former will lead to more disputes while the latter will create lasting improvements.

Physical possessions can be a front for self-esteem too, as glittering with gold won't prevent us from feeling poor in spirit. Status symbols can be equally suspicious, as having a magazine-modeling husband won't inhibit us from feeling ugly inside. Accolades can be empty too, as the top surgeon at Stanford isn't immune from insecurity about their skills. Prada handbags, trophy wives, and hard-earned PhDs can be superficial check-marks that appear to be self-esteem signals when they're merely facades.

There's nothing wrong with having a house in the hills or a distinguished award for your career achievements. These marks of accomplishment can do wonders for our self-confidence because they feel damn good. However, high self-esteem means feeling good whether we have these things or not. If we base our teaching abilities on the prestige of the institution we're working for, we're probably chasing self-confidence. If we love to teach and care more about transferring knowledge than the ratio of Ivy League-destined pupils in our classrooms, we're likely operating with self-esteem.

Defining Self-Esteem

Self-esteem is defined as feeling good about ourselves because we accept who we are. We don't need to prop up our self-esteem on impressive socioeconomic statuses, accolades from local clubs, or abilities to perform Mozart. We can bolster our self-confidence through symbols of status, but they won't always lead to self-esteem. Having a glow of self-esteem means being positive about our positions in life, whether we're CEOs or sanitation service workers.

Beyond status, having self-esteem means accepting our strengths and weaknesses without pride, shame, or deflection. A person with self-esteem can look at themselves in the mirror and say, "I break out in fits of violence when I drink alcohol. I'm not ashamed to acknowledge this ugly side of me and I know I would have better relationships with others if I didn't drink at all." While this person has problematic behavior under the influence, they accept it without misgivings and can rationalize a way to live a healthier life. If they had low self-esteem they might wallow in pity, proclaiming, "I'm a drunken failure who can't be happy without alcohol, and I'm throwing my life away getting into bar fights every night. Woe is me!"

When it comes to strengths, a person with low self-esteem might puff their chest at their own reflection and say, "I'm a star because I'm the top-performing dancer in the country. Anyone who thinks otherwise has no idea what they're talking about. If you're not the best at what you do, you don't deserve to talk to me." This person appears to be a strong dancer, but they place their entire self-worth on their ability to perform. They are resistant to criticism and would feel attacked if someone disagreed with their outlook. Without their prestigious position, they might value themselves less as a person. If they had higher self-esteem, their opinion might be "Dancing brings me joy because I love participating in the art form. Even if I weren't good enough to perform on Broadway, I'd still enjoy practicing on a small stage."

Demonstrating self-esteem requires two steps. The first step is to look at our strengths, weaknesses, and position in life with honesty. The second step is to accept those qualities about ourselves without a coping mechanism like deflection, delusion, or dramatization. If we can perform these two steps, we can feel good about ourselves no matter what.

However, gazing into the mirror can be uncomfortable, especially when we don't know how to honestly evaluate our negative feelings, unhealthy behaviors, and subconscious attractions. It would be easier to paint the mirror black and etch "You look great!" on the surface. That might boost our self-confidence in the moment, but if we lacked self-esteem, doubt would inevitably creep in. The longer we go without truly knowing ourselves, the more an uneasy feeling will gnaw at us from the inside. We'll feel the urge to scratch off the facade and see whether we're really as "great" as the inscription claims. We cannot paint over our low self-esteem with the darkest inks or the most brilliant self-affirmations. We have to face our inner truth eventually.

4

Building Authentic Self-Esteem

President John Fitzgerald Kennedy and First Lady Jacqueline Lee Kennedy had one of the most scrutinized relationships of all time. Their affairs, remarriages, and tragedies were always in the public eye during their lifetimes. Famously, President Kennedy stated he would get terrible headaches if he didn't have sex for three days, and he entertained a parade of mistresses during his time in the Oval Office. Jackie knew about her husband's promiscuous activity and once remarked, "He's like my father in a way—loves the chase and is bored with the conquest—and, once married, needs proof he's still attractive, so flirts with other women and resents you."

Jackie played the perfect First Lady in her elegance, bravery, and complacency with her husband's affairs. She made jokes to assistants in passing about the women John was supposedly sleeping with, but never displayed frustration in public. She attempted to keep her personal life out of the public eye as much as possible, however, her self-esteem appears to have been tied to the worldly status of her men. Her first husband, President Kennedy, her second husband, Aristotle Onassis, and her lifelong partner, Maurice Templesman, were each magnates, and among the most powerful men of their time.

A widow at only 34, Jackie Kennedy waited five years and then remarried Greek shipping tycoon Aristotle Onassis. The public was uncomfortable with the world-famous widow choosing another husband after JFK's assassination. Perhaps the American people would have been more approving if she picked anyone other than Onassis.

On the surface, her relationship with Onassis seemed improper. They were married in an Orthodox church instead of a Catholic church, Onassis' ex-wife was still alive, and Aristotle wasn't even *American*. These taboos compounded with a significant age difference (Jackie was thirty-nine and Aristotle was sixty-two), a swath of close friends who considered the two incompatible, and a messy history that resembles a high-profile love quadrangle.

A few months prior to JFK's assassination, Jackie Kennedy's sister Lee Radziwill invited her to attend Onassis' yacht voyage in the Aegean Sea. According to Secret Service agent Clint Hill, John F. Kennedy forbade Jackie to "cross paths with Aristotle Onassis," as he was concerned by Aristotle's history of affairs with world-famous women. The president reportedly didn't like the idea of the trip, fearing it would appear improper. But he relented.

In *Nemesis: The True Story*, Peter Evans states one of Onassis' flings was with Jackie's sister. Meanwhile JFK's brother Robert was in a business grudge with Onassis and shared contempt for the shipping tycoon. A few months after the president's assassination, FBI documents report evidence of Bobby Kennedy and Jackie Kennedy being lovers. Bobby's hate for Onassis compounded when Aristotle dated Jackie. He frequently tried to prevent the two from marrying until 1968 when an assassin with ties to Onassis shot him dead.

"Not a single friend thought Jackie should marry Onassis," Evans wrote. "But now that Bobby was gone, there was no one who could stop her."

Four months after Bobby's assassination, Jackie remarried on Onassis' private island, Skorpios, and she would forever become "Jackie O." The New York Times wrote, "The reaction here is anger, shock, and dismay."

It's easy to believe Jackie married Onassis because he was one of the richest men in the world and could provide her the security, status, and socialite lifestyle she desired. Onassis likely married Jackie because as the widow of JFK and ex-lover of his nemesis, Bobby, she was the ultimate trophy wife. Biographers unanimously agree Onassis and Jackie didn't love each other. Jackie herself said Onassis "Rescued me at a moment when my life was engulfed in shadows" and "The first time you marry for love, the second for money, and the third for companionship."

From JFK's endless affairs and Jackie's diverse marriages a pattern of false conscious attractions emerges. Both were highly successful political figures, with high levels of self-confidence. But their jumps from one relationship to the next indicate low levels of self-esteem as they searched for authentic connection and emotional gratification. JFK relied on frequently bedding new women to boost his self-confidence and fill his need for connection. Naturally, these surface level relationships did not offer lasting Mercury Mind connections. Similar to her late husband, but using a different method, Jackie entered into relationships with powerful men to boost her self confidence. It seems being close to power made Jackie feel important and served to quell her insecurity regarding the fulfillment of rigid standards of behavior for women.

Both Kennedys relied on self-confidence, and continually refueled with inadequate relationships, stirred up controversies, and alleged assassinations. Neither Kennedy could find true Mercury Mind connections until they developed self-esteem.

In the years after Onassis's death, Jackie seems to have finally found a Mercury Mind connection. She eventually obtained the loving companionship she so desperately sought with Maurice Tempelsman, a diamond merchant. They never married, but lived together in New York City, enjoying walks together in Central Park. They were devoted to each other until her death in 1994.

Self-confidence is short-lived, but self-esteem can last a lifetime. We think self-confidence will make us feel better about ourselves, but it is as fleeting as a jolt of courage from a motivational poster hanging outside a doctor's office. It's fragile and needs constant refueling—usually in the form of achieving our conscious plans—to stoke its flames.

It appears that JFK refueled his self-confidence with constant sexual attention. He had an intelligent, fashionista, role-model wife, but his low self-esteem meant he needed constant boosts from lots of other people. His sense of worth was tied to what other people thought of him. He was the leader of the free world and one of the most beloved Presidents of all time according to Gallup, but his behavior demonstrates a toxic attraction toward gaining validation from sleeping with women infatuated with him. This suggests low levels of self-esteem. His wife's love and a nation of fervorous supporters didn't reassure him, so he sought evermore ego-stroking from frequent sex. JFK chased self-confidence on a daily basis, but had he developed self-esteem instead, he might have found a Mercury Mind connection that would allow him to sleep soundly at night and accomplish the goals he had for the nation. With higher self-esteem, JFK might have had an authentic Mercury Mind connection with Jackie Kennedy or with another partner altogether. He could have enjoyed a deeper, more fulfilling relationship because he was secure and comfortable in his own worth and wouldn't need to chase girls for validation.

Self-esteem is the foundation for healthy relationships, not self-confidence. JFK appeared self-confident in speeches, campaigns, and press events, but never achieved stable self-confidence. He faked it but never made it. Self-esteem breeds stable self-confidence, but no amount of self-confidence can increase self-esteem.

Self-esteem is a self-perpetuating engine. Once it gets going, it's hard to stop and doesn't need constant refueling to make us feel good. If we feel great about our strengths, weaknesses, and position every day, we won't need cheap dates or other fleeting reassurances to be self-confident. Instead, our ever-blooming self-esteem will allow us to take honest looks in the mirror without shame, guilt, or deflection. With better evaluations of ourselves, we can accept we're doing well and what we need to work on. Self-acceptance in turn feeds our self-esteem, and the cycle continues. Forget about fueling the fire every day like JFK. We can build a self-esteem engine that lasts a lifetime.

Hard Work Beats Out the Quick Fix

We want to believe confidence-building tactics work because these quick-fix strategies appeal to our desire to abate uncertainty and avoid the long, painful, and ambiguous work of accepting ourselves. Self-confidence only requires us to learn a few tricks or buy a few gadgets to bolster our self-image.

In contrast to self-confidence, self-esteem requires vulnerability. Vulnerability is an openness to uncertainty, which allows us to sit with our open cycles long enough to let them come to a natural conclusion. A side effect of hating uncertainty is that we avoid vulnerability and we neglect nurturing our self-esteem.

Humans favor the easier path of constant confidence reinforcement even though it requires more energy and lower reward over the long-term. This pattern is congruent with our desire for instant gratification in lieu of long-term satisfaction. In the infamous marshmallow test,[1] children were offered two options: a) eat the marshmallow on the table in front of them while the researcher was out of the test room, or b) wait ten minutes for the researcher to return to the room and eat two marshmallows. Despite the greater reward, only 30% of children were able to delay gratification. The attraction to sweet certainty is greater than trusting the stranger in the white coat for a double-dose of *Stay-Puft* satisfaction.

We can see many examples of this gravitation toward instant gratification in our everyday interactions. A woman chooses to chow down on a burger, which tastes better in the moment, instead of opting for the salad, which would lower her cholesterol and boost her energy in the long term. A man decides to masturbate to the model in the workout video instead of waiting to connect with the real person he's going on a date with later that night. Uncle Gary prefers to proffer opinions on the environment culled from Facebook memes instead of reading the publicly available Intergovernmental Panel on

Climate Change report, which would give him a greater understanding and ability to argue his points.

Like resisting the temptation of a tasty treat, or taking the time to gather reputable facts before posting about our thoughts, patience often pays off later. In fact, there is a strong correlation between delayed gratification and higher self-esteem, better relationships, greater emotional intelligence, psychological well-being, and overall achievement.[2] Conversely, people who chose instant over delayed gratification are more likely to be involved with illicit activities, perform worse academically, and suffer from a poorer self-image.[3]

Not only does instant gratification correlate with undesirable long-term outcomes, but it's also associated with a false sense of confidence. A 2016 study looking at hubristic pride versus authentic pride in the role of gratification found individuals whose pride was rooted in prosocial achievement rather than self-aggrandizement were able to delay satisfaction and reap greater rewards.[4] In other words, to sit in uncertainty and delay gratification means we will be more likely to work toward true benefits rather than empty self-confidence.

We are taught to favor the instant gratification of certain confidence over the delayed gratification of developing self-esteem. In order to surpass our innate impulses, we must train ourselves to look beyond our fixations of the moment to the potential reward of the future.

It may feel insurmountable to overcome our natural impulses for the instant gratification of self-confidence, but there is a mechanism to help us practice delayed gratification. This practice involves setting our sights on the long-term rather than grasping for an immediate reward. By adopting a future-oriented mindset, studies show we are able to effectively delay gratification and work toward authentic long-term goals.[5]

When we face uncertainty and let our cycles stay open instead of relying on quick-fix confidence boosters and false conscious plans, we can set our sights on the long-term goal of letting our self-esteem grow organically. Through embracing the development of our self-esteem, we are able to create a self-perpetuating machine that sustains our sense of self through the uncertainty of life and relationships. We can make friends with our insecurity and fall in love with the flawed person we are.

Developing a sense of comfort with ourselves leads to the stabilization of our Mercury Minds, which allows us to truly connect with our desires, others, and the world and people around us. More plainly, becoming OK with our insecurities allows for true intimacy with ourselves and others. For many, this intangible benefit is difficult to grasp compared to the concrete and quantifiable accomplishments we can obtain by following our conscious plans and striving for self-confidence. However, it is ultimately a deep sense of self-worth that will lead us down the road of authentic, unassailable happiness, not an accomplishment, accolade, or partner.

The ancient Greek philosopher Epicurus was often labeled as a hedonist because of his emphasis on pursuing pleasure over pain. When we think of an ancient Grecian hedonist, we might envisage a person lying on a velvet couch being fed grapes by a half-naked servant. However, this was far from Epicurus's vision. Epicurus believed pleasure should be the ultimate destination. Thus, he thought we should avoid actions that lead to pain, even if they are pleasurable in the moment.[6] If temporary pain and discomfort lead to happiness down the line, as is the case with working out, then Epicurus would be in favor. Moreover, the pain is easier to get through if we see it as a means to an end.

The key to a more fulfilling life is doing the hard work of coming to terms with who we honestly are.

Why We Dodge Self-Esteem Development

Understanding the importance of self-esteem is not enough to inspire us to develop it. Often, we are held back by low self-esteem and this causes us to feel sorry for ourselves. When we look in the mirror we tell ourselves we aren't good enough and throw in the towel before attempting to improve, due to the overwhelming feeling of uncertainty that change would bring.

Developing self-esteem requires vulnerability, which can be

uncomfortable. Acknowledging our flaws can make us nervous if we aren't accustomed to self-critique. It's much easier to pretend we're flawless than to let our guard down and dig into our inadequacies. Further, accepting our shortcomings means opening our cycles, which can make us uneasy. When we suddenly face a barrage of open cycles, we might fall into depression, denial, or anxiety and do anything we can think of to close the cycles. We cannot improve all our weaknesses by greeting them, sleeping on them, and putting them in the "done" pile when we wake up. We must be patient to break our unhealthy behaviors, practice new ways to fulfill our attractions, and wait for open cycles to close naturally. If we cannot sit with our inadequacies, we cannot develop self-esteem.

Of course, all of this is assuming we can even identify our weaknesses and attractions in the first place, and discover healthy ways to improve. Most of us don't know who we are inside, especially if we've avoided self-reflection for a long time. It can be incredibly difficult to put a finger on our weak spots, our subconscious attractions, and our next best steps. We fear the unknown within, so we either stop ourselves from working on our self-esteem as soon as we encounter something unfamiliar, or we fill in the unknown parts of ourselves with biased answers to rapidly ameliorate the uncertainty. This can make us unreliable agents for our own self-esteem development. For this reason, we often need outside help from a counselor to fact-check our self-analyses before we go about implementing our self-improvement regimes. This adds another barrier as many of us are afraid of spilling our guts in front of a professional. Existing low self-esteem, fear of vulnerability, and avoidance of uncertainty are all reasons we dodge self-esteem development.

Gauging Self-Esteem

The mistakes we're making in our personal relationships can help us gauge our self-esteem levels. Take the example of dating the "wrong" people. There are those of us who frequently find ourselves in disrespectful relationships and seem to put up with the poor treatment. When we feel we've had enough of one awful relationship, we start dating someone new who yells at us, plays mind games, lies, and cheats to cause physical harm. Any one of these red flags should signal the relationship is unhealthy, yet many of us continuously date "bad boys" or "black widow spiders" who step all over us. One reason we find ourselves with the "wrong" people is our low self-esteem. If we believe we are unworthy of being treated in a healthy way, we will put up with unhealthy relationships.

People who struggle with relationships often minimize *why* they end up with troublesome people or find themselves dumped by those they adore. We come up with superficial excuses like "I'm not tall enough," or "I don't have big enough breasts," or "I attract people who don't like who I am." It's convenient to boil our problems down to something as simple and uncontrollable as our height. It's confidence-building to claim we're all superstars who deserve the moon, but no one else seems to notice. These illusions about our frequent relationship troubles represent low self-esteem, a lack of honest self-reflection, and deflection onto others rather than noticing patterns in our own actions.

Consequently, when we have low self-esteem we latch on to relationships with red flags. We beg our problematic partners to stay with us because we're so afraid of being alone and having to face our inadequacies. We use relationships as evidence of our self-worth rather than developing self-esteem independently. We value having *any* romantic relationship over having a *quality* relationship. Suddenly, we find ourselves stuck in another dead-end, unhealthy, inauthentic relationship for the umpteenth time. At this point we could develop our self-esteem by turning the mirror inward and considering that we might be the repeat offenders. Or, we could perpetuate our low self-esteem by deflecting the blame, conjuring a superficial excuse, and pretending we deserve better.

When we have low self-esteem, we unknowingly sabotage ourselves with painful relationships. We become unhappy and might react to our difficult feelings by taking drugs, jumping into new relationships, or using a complex of other coping mechanisms. We tell ourselves "This isn't fair," "I'm better than this," or "I don't deserve this treatment," but dissatisfaction is exactly what we earn when we have low self-esteem.

A person with high self-esteem would walk away from a demeaning relationship right away. They wouldn't put up with someone who isn't an authentic fit. They would accept themselves fully, whether they were in a relationship or not. They would experience emotional gratification from within instead of basing their happiness on a relationship status.

When we can generate satisfaction within ourselves, we can attract other like-minded people who engage with us through authentic Mercury Mind connections. When we have high self-esteem we realize that we *do* deserve better than toxicity.

There are a few strategies we will cover in later chapters that will help us become more comfortable with the parts of ourselves that we might think don't measure up. One such strategy is the practice of vulnerability. But first we have to look at how dodging self-esteem development is tied into our troubles with intimacy.

How We Avoid Intimacy

While developing authentic self-esteem is an important step in achieving intimacy, before we adopt this mindset we must first understand the mechanisms we employ to avoid true intimacy. We distort the world through a circle of idealization and devaluation. This allows us to shape our reality in a way that makes us more confident. This illusion makes it easier to force intimacy, instead of being vulnerable and honest with ourselves to arrive at intimacy naturally.

If you have to lie to yourself or others to achieve intimacy, your "intimate" relationships will be fragile. They will fall apart in time because they are built on false pretenses. Sometimes these connections can even become toxic.

We feel insecure about intimacy because it requires vulnerability, which means our perceived flaws might come to light. In order to circumvent this, we fixate on people who we believe can give us the feeling of intimacy we crave, without having to be vulnerable. Often, we idealize these people because it is easier to construct a narrative that we believe fulfills our needs than to accept others (and ourselves) as they truly are, flaws and all. This often leads to stereotypes, misjudgment, and a gross overvaluation of others and undervaluation of ourselves.

Through confidence-building techniques, we may be able to attain the object of our desire. When this happens, though, we often find ourselves disappointed. Since the script we've created around that person is constructed to reflect what we think we need out of them, the chances of our partner playing their part to our expectations is low. When our predetermined script isn't followed, we feel pain and disconnection. Armed with our confidence and our frustration that our new relationships don't meet our expectations, we create reasons why the other person is the problem. We devalue our partners and overvalue ourselves.

In the Netflix series *You*, the main character, Joe, is an extreme example of this pattern. Joe, a man who suffered from a lack of close and nurturing connections in his youth, desperately craves intimacy. He develops a pattern, which he repeats multiple times throughout the series. He fixates on a particular woman to the point of stalking her. He idealizes this woman as the ultimate solution to his loneliness. He believes she is perfect in every way for him, despite the fact he knows little about her beyond his superficial observations. He narrates a fairy tale story in which he is the prince coming to save her from an unsatisfying and fractured existence. Ultimately, he creates a relationship with her using the knowledge he's attained from his reconnaissance. When, through the course of a relationship, she begins to display traits that aren't congruent with his idealized version of her, he begins to devalue her. Eventually, the woman also reaches a point of seeing past the role he is playing, and finds she has been manipulated. A confrontation ensues, usually leading to the woman's untimely death at Joe's hands. Joe walks away confident the woman was the wrong-doer. The pattern repeats.

For most of us, we do not take our narratives to the extreme of Joe, but many of us do face a repeating circle of idealization and devaluation. This is not only present in our romantic relationships, but also in our relationships with parents, friends, and business partners.

This circle even appears in our relationships with our careers, objects, and spirituality. This is why someone who raves about their new church one day can condemn it the following week as the nexus of evil. It's why someone who works eighty hours a week to make partner at their law firm can suddenly find they hate their job when their name is plastered on the business logo. It's why we rebel against our upbringing when we find out our parents are flawed people just like us. Our confidence is brought into question when reality is exposed and we must choose between letting our confidence crumble in the face of our illusions, or clinging to unrealistic expectations.

If we choose the option to let our confidence be dismantled when our idealizations are proven to be just that, we may not immediately proceed with seeking vulnerability and connection. Alternatively, we may decide to create unattainable idealizations so our illusions aren't threatened. In creating these unreachable objects of desire, we feel temporary confidence in our affections, mimicking a feeling of intimacy.

At the same time, a false sense of intimacy gives us a hollow shell of confidence. If we are obsessed with Hugh Jackman, we may feel like we know him through his movies, interviews, and endearing Instagram dance videos, but there is little chance Hugh Jackman knows or cares about us. Over time, while we staunchly grasp onto our obsessions, we feel increasingly dissatisfied because we lack intimacy. We have not managed to create Mercury Mind connections with others and we end up dissatisfied both in our conscious and subconscious goals. Over time, this degrades the confidence we once gained from being superfan #1 and we devalue ourselves with increasing vigor.

Idealization may be initially easier than true vulnerability, but it is the enemy of authentic Mercury Mind connections. When we release idealizations, we may have to face two hard truths: 1) that we haven't really formed a bond at all, with anyone and (2) we only have ourselves to blame for it. Since we forged a connection to feel intimacy, it might not stem from a real magnetism, but from our need to feed our confidence. Maybe we deserve to be in the dissatisfied position we are in because we have not done the work to create authentic connection. In order to develop a true Mercury Mind connection, we must be vulnerable enough to let ourselves and others be what we are outside of a script.

Vulnerability is the Key

Once we understand how we avoid intimacy, we must turn our sights to a pathway toward developing authentic self-esteem. Intimacy relies on our capacity to accept ourselves and others in our authentic form. In order to gain this acceptance, we must cultivate vulnerability and let our lives float into the unknown.

Vulnerability is rooted in relinquishing control. However, we have a deep desire to control everything in our lives. We want to feel confidence because it makes the uncertain seem certain. But control is no match for the elemental force of our Mercury Mind, which is beyond our control. There is only one path that can withstand the monumental pressure of our subconscious desires. That path is release.

A confidence-only approach will leave us stranded in the end. Just as we need to feed fuel into the engine to keep the car running, we need to continually bolster our confidence from the outside. When it runs out, we are forced to stop before ever reaching the destination we seek. The longer we try to control our dating lives through the *How to Beast* handbook, the less effective these strategies are. Eventually, it leads to a fiery *crash, bang, boom!* and we are left alone once again.

We may think the simple solution is to feed our self-esteem instead of our confidence, but self-esteem, unlike confidence, is not something we can consciously control. Instead, we can only attain self-esteem through the long, challenging pathway of letting ourselves be who we are in absolute. It's only when we fully accept and become OK with ourselves as we are that we gain true self-esteem.

The antithesis to confidence is not self-esteem. The opposite of confidence is release. We must release our need to control and allow our true selves to come to the surface. This builds authentic self-esteem and naturally attracts more Mercury Mind connections into our orbit.

If we turn away from the mirror as soon as we catch an ugly visage, we cement the impression that we're "not good enough." And we'll never find that feeling of wholeness if we shun ourselves because of our perceived flaws. It is okay to have weaknesses—no one can be good at everything. Self-esteem is built on acceptance of who we are, just as we are. This does not mean we can't strive to change a part of ourselves that we'd like to improve. Working on ourselves doesn't mean we are somehow broken or bad. In fact, working on ourselves proves to us and others that we are worthy of our own time and attention. When we value ourselves, others begin to gravitate toward us.

We might use confidence-based rules to superficially alter what we see in the mirror, hiding our strengths and weaknesses from ourselves. Doing this takes us further away from our authentic selves as we become like chameleons ready to change at a moment's notice in order to live up to standards set by other people, society, and the economy. We change so much of who we are, we lose touch with our authentic Mercury Mind foundation and can't build the relationships we're attracted to in healthy ways. The more we dodge self-esteem development, the more we'll struggle to realize our natural attractions. Our fear of vulnerability bites us.

Vulnerability can be uncomfortable, but learning to face ourselves honestly is the first step in seeing ourselves as enough. When we accept our authentic selves, we can forge self-esteem and make authentic connections with others. We must be transparent with our vulnerabilities because acting as chameleons who build relationships on false pretenses will lead us to inauthentic relationships. The more genuine our connections with others, the more others will feel connected to us. They will understand our reactions, our humor, and our deepest desires. They won't be repelled by our true natures because we've established authenticity from the start. Never again will we play a charade to win friends and influence people. On the contrary, our authentic actions will bring others closer to us, reinforcing bonds. Those who do not accept us for our strengths and weaknesses will sever ties, which is a benefit for us because those relationships would have been destined to become toxic. We don't want to spend our lives entangled in shallow, short-lived, inauthentic relationships with those who do not appreciate who we are. All of this is possible if we first learn how to be vulnerable and view ourselves with unabashed and critical reflections.

But before we dive into building our self-esteem generators, let's evaluate how vulnerability affects the various relationships in our lives…

5

Finding True Connection in Relationships

With over seventy battles won in his name,[1] Napoleon Bonaparte had one of the most tactical minds in military history. Generals remember him as being like a chess master, planning his next checkmate ten moves ahead. Napoleon spoke of his battles with a mechanistic mind.[2] In the 1806 Battle of Auerstadt, the forces of Prussia outnumbered the French by more than double. When King William III of Prussia was informed Napoleon led the opposing charge, however, he retreated despite his immense advantage.[3] Napoleon's name carried enough weight that no one wanted to face him on the battlefield.

Yet, Napoleon was also known for his inability to accept defeat and his dogged rejection of criticism. The great general cheated at cards because he couldn't shoulder the loss.[4] He was so terrified of being perceived as weak, he negotiated strong-armed treaties with other countries rather than offering true peace and a chance for alliance.[5] When Napoleon's wife Josephine routinely cheated on him, he issued the sexist Napoleonic Code instead of expressing his hurt feelings to her.[6] The code stated that a man could murder his wife for cheating on him, while a man's infidelity would only incur a small fine. Napoleon knew his wife was sleeping around, but his staunch commitment to his image of himself as a god didn't reconcile with the reality of a man who was a cuckold.

Napoleon's myopic view of himself was impenetrable. He shied away from vulnerability, making him a subject of derision today. Napoleon was fragile because he based his self-image on battlefield wins, fear from other nations, and accolades from his own people.

Deep down, Napoleon wanted to belong and be loved. In his youth, he was routinely bullied for his family's low economic standing.[7] He spent years climbing the ladder to eventually join the ranks of the elite, simultaneously adoring and despising the upper classes along the way. When he couldn't find an organic pathway to belonging, he opted for domination. He was obsessed with power, and believed it would bring him the affection he craved. However, his need for control did not bring belonging—it brought exile. His inability to be vulnerable isolated him from possible Mercury Mind connections.

Napoleon's life and legacy demonstrate once again that self-confidence is a poor substitute for authenticity. When we choose to pump up our confidence instead of accepting our flaws, we risk destroying our relationships. In contrast, vulnerability draws people closer to us.

Zach Galifinakis, a few inches taller than Napoleon, is well-loved by the American public. On *Conan O'Brien* in 2005, Galifinakis sat in a brown velvet suit and played the piano with the ease of a Vegas crooner.[8] He didn't talk about how good he was at the piano. He didn't try to act tough. Instead, he made fun of himself.

"I went to my high school reunion not too long ago, and that was… something. I was homeschooled," Zach recalled with a self-derisive glance at the ivory keys. He continued, "So it was just me standing next to a bowl of punch listening to Cool n' the Gang, talking about how fat I've gotten. I have gotten fatter, which sucks because I'm claustrophobic."

Zach Galifinakis wasn't lauded by his peers in his youth. He was bullied because of his height.[9] In turn, he admitted to bullying others in retaliation. The difference between Napoleon and Zach Galifinakis is the path they took as adults.

We love Zach Galifinakis because he lets us see who he is. He owns his insecurity about his plumpness, awkwardness, and short stature. He is not afraid to share these qualities through his jokes. He may not like his flaws, but he maintains a strong enough self-esteem to let himself be seen as he authentically is. It is this vulnerability that bonds audiences to him.

While Zach chose to take responsibility for his participation in the bullying cycle, Napoleon took retaliation to the extreme and led a revolution culminating in a reign of terror. Between the comedian and the military leader, Galifinakis is the one who we could see ourselves being friends with.

Vulnerability Is Key

Exposing our imperfections requires vulnerability, which leaves us open to rejection. The truth is it's hard to sustain healthy, long-term relationships without allowing ourselves to be open about our flaws and insecurities. When we cultivate vulnerability we gain the capacity for self-acceptance through an organic understanding, which ultimately leads to higher self-esteem. And a strong sense of self-esteem is the key to healthy relationships, because it helps us draw other people to us who are also vulnerable and comfortable with their flaws and insecurities. Once we accept ourselves, we can better accept others as they are. At the same time, we do not want to compromise our healthy value system in order to achieve connection. Attractions must be organic. Through sharing our vulnerabilities, we create mutual intimacy and gain the love and belonging we desire.

To understand the difference, consider two hypothetical couples: Couple A and Couple B.

Couple A is a pair of college students who have been together for six months. They are young and in love, but wildly insecure. The boy is fresh off a high school tenure that featured daily bouts of bullying. He wants to show the girl how "cool" he is, so he takes her out to expensive dinners and Ed Sheeran concerts he can't afford. The girl struggles with self-image issues she doesn't want to share with her new beau, so she secretly vomits after every steak dinner and berates herself for not being as pretty as the other girls at the concert. Both are afraid the other will think less of them if they share their weaknesses. However, without these admissions, their relationship will disintegrate as the boy runs out of money and the girl faces serious health consequences. Eventually, they will likely grow to resent each other.

Couple B features another pair of university students who have been dating for six months. The woman was bullied in high school for being a nerd. The man struggled for years with body image and feelings of low self-worth. The female has embraced her nerd-hood upon arriving at campus. She is studying to become a computer engineer and hosts weekly D&D nights. The male allowed himself to be vulnerable and seek help, becoming an advocate for healthy self-image among teen boys. The girl feels socially awkward sometimes, and the boy feels anxious about having too much cake, but neither hides their insecurities. They embrace their flaws, resolved or not. This shared awareness and acceptance allows them to feel connected and supported. This acceptance leads to love, instead of isolation.

To connect with another person, we must first be vulnerable with ourselves. If we cannot accept our struggles, we cannot hope to be intimate with another person.

In our anxiety over uncertainty, we often try to skip ahead. We forgo the painful process of facing ourselves and jump straight into a forced sense of intimacy. We try to create a feeling of connection through roses, weekend getaways, or long nights talking about who we want to be instead of who we are. These romantic endeavors can make us feel good temporarily, but they are not the bedrock of an authentic connection.

Vulnerability and Beyond

Hallmark rom-com elements are not the basis for a real connection, so we must look deeper to uncover the secret to true lasting relationships. Vulnerability, self-acceptance, and self-esteem are necessary components of intimacy. However, not everyone who is authentic and vulnerable will be automatically drawn toward each other. Natural intimacy is in rooted four sources:

- Vulnerability
- Genuine Mercury Mind connection
- Similar level of self-esteem
- Shared values

All four sources must be present to make a relationship work, but none of the four are enough on their own. Vulnerability is only the first of four critical ingredients for true intimacy. The second ingredient is a genuine Mercury Mind connection.

Mercury Mind Connection

The Mercury Mind is the elemental force that pulls us into relationships. It is an indescribable feeling of attraction. It is an unknowable and irresistible magnetism that draws us like moths to a flame. Even if two people are both vulnerable, they can't develop the highest level of true love without a genuine Mercury Mind connection. The Mercury Mind is responsible for those connections we feel that outsiders may not understand. It is how a Republican big game hunter can end up dating a vegan Democrat. It's how a millionaire supermodel can marry a poor, portly, balding man. It is how a Christian minister and a pagan witch can run off to Bermuda and start a life together. Mercury Mind connections are not inhibited by labels, they are beautifully inexplicable attractions that we cannot consciously control.

Likewise, a lack of Mercury Mind connection is why we sometimes find that people who seem like they should connect, do not. This is why two genuine and vulnerable people with similar values may find they have nothing to talk about and no desire to engage with each other. It's why you can hook up two friends who seem perfect for each other only to hear they didn't feel a "spark." It's why you can think someone seems amazing based on their online dating profile only to find you don't connect when you meet for coffee. This lack of natural attraction demonstrates that some pairs are incompatible. The

Mercury Mind does not work based on surface level similarities, it is and always will be mysterious.

On the other hand, while a Mercury Mind connection is necessary for a real attraction, it isn't sufficient on its own for a relationship to last the test of time. If a relationship is based on a Mercury Mind connection without any other substance, it can deteriorate quickly. The vegan may resent the hunter for killing animals. The portly, balding man may feel insecure and cheat on his supermodel girlfriend. The Christian and the pagan may hide their respective faiths from each other and never achieve a deep level of intimacy.

High Self-Esteem

Self-esteem is closely tied to our level of self-acceptance. We are often drawn to other people with a comparable level of self-esteem as our own. Therefore, two people with low self-esteem might find themselves attracted to each other, but because they do not accept themselves, they will find it challenging to accept each other. In lieu of this genuine acceptance, they'll scramble to instill confidence in themselves and their relationship. However, confidence is always temporary. Over time, their discomfort with themselves will surface and poison the relationship.

For example, a woman who feels unworthy of love may be attracted to a man who feels undeserving of a healthy relationship. The woman may cling desperately to any display of attraction. The man may dismiss and abuse his partner. Both can easily grow to resent the other.

Similarly, a person with high self-esteem and a partner with low self-esteem may feel mismatched. If a man who loathes the fact that he is gay dates a man who is comfortable with his sexuality, the first man may need constant validation of his masculinity. The second can quickly feel drained by this and end the relationship out of exhaustion.

Shared Values

Imagine a Christian minister and pagan witch who have vulnerability, a Mercury Mind connection, and comparably high levels of self-esteem. They may authentically share who they are and connect on a deeply unknowable level, but they might not sustain a relationship if they have different values. A Christian minister who holds traditional views on marriage and a pagan witch who hosts naked dance parties in the woods may hold conflicting ethics. At moral odds, they need a compromise in values or a split. However, compromising our values can deteriorate our authenticity. When we trade away who we are for another person, the relationship suffers.

Testing Our Existing Relationships

After learning to recognize the essential components of a healthy attraction, we can evaluate our existing relationships to see whether they meet the standard for a lasting connection. This framework applies to all types of relationships. The need for intimacy is not limited to a romantic or sexual context, but shows up in friendships, business partnerships, careers, and even our relationships with material possessions. Intimacy in any kind of relationship, with anyone or anything, requires vulnerability and authenticity. For example, it's hard to have a deep and meaningful friendship if we never reveal our struggles with alcohol addiction to the other person. Similarly, to develop a profound connection with a mentor at work we must be genuinely interested in the other person, not just in what they can do for us. On the other hand, if we rebuild a vintage Ford convertible over the years, we must authentically enjoy the car for the feeling it gives us when we are working on it alone in the garage. If we are only clinging to the vehicle for the sake of a status symbol, it is likely feeding our confidence, not our self-esteem.

We are attracted to relationships for a variety of reasons. We may admire a boss, desire to mentor a child, or feel like a big-screen TV fills a missing part within us. Whether these attractions are healthy depends on our capacity to sustain them.

To test our existing relationships, we can start by asking ourselves a few questions.

- Do you feel an organic attraction toward this person/object?

- Would you be excited to hang out with this person/object in any place and in any dynamic?
- If you are relying on this person to give you something or take you somewhere in your life, would you still care about them if they couldn't provide you with what you wanted?
- Would you be willing to risk rejection to share embarrassing or painful truths about yourself?
- How do you feel about yourself when you are around that person or object?
- Do the values of this person/object align with your authentic values?

Sometimes, it may be too early in a relationship to answer these questions. In those cases, we feel a strong attraction to someone or something but we aren't sure how deep that feeling really is. Through following these attractions and observing ourselves and our partners in the relationship, we can gain the ability to answer these questions over time. Eventually we will be able to articulate why we are drawn to a particular relationship and whether the feeling is sustainable.

The Three Types of Relationships

There are three main categories of relationships we all encounter in our lives. Each category comes with its own rewards and pitfalls. There are healthy and unhealthy patterns for each type of relationship and by understanding them we can learn to develop more authentic connections.

- Business partnerships
- Non-romantic connections, which can include friendships and familial relationships
- Romantic relationships

Business Relationships

In the business world, we have relationships with customers, associates, bosses, co-workers, mentors, and mentees. Business partnerships can either be superficial or authentic, which creates two categories: transactional connections and partnerships.

Transactional connections are based on *quid pro quo*. I give you a product or perform a service for you, and you give me money in exchange. These relationships do not require a Mercury Mind connection, vulnerability, self-esteem, or shared values to be successful because they are temporary by nature. On the other hand, long-standing partnerships must be based on an intimate connection.

On a conscious level we might be drawn to a certain coworker because they are linked to status, products, or people we want to connect with. Similarly, we can be captivated by people in business because they embody what we want to be. We may mistake our feelings of envy for attraction. When we glorify a business associate we devalue ourselves in the process. This creates distance between us and our associates, and pulls us further away from authentic attractions. We overvalue qualities we don't possess and devalue ourselves for not having them.

Though the traps of idealization and devaluation are common pitfalls in business relationships, this does not mean we are consigned to only develop deep relationships with peers. It is possible to form healthy, intimate connections with bosses and mentors if participating individuals are genuine in who they are and their respect for each other.

In a business context, an authentic relationship means each party recognizes their own and each other's flaws. Moreover, they call each other out freely on mistakes, and accept each other's judgments without resentment. They embrace their differences and celebrate everyone's unique contributions. In business, bringing together different specializations can help a company run efficiently. If we had ten people in a business who were good at marketing and two who were adept at accounting, we wouldn't try to force the accountants to become marketers. We would embrace the accountants for the value they bring. The same is true with the more intangible qualities of our business partners. When we can see ourselves and others honestly, we can develop more authentic relationships.

To consider whether a business relationship is healthy, ask whether it is transactional or long-term. If it is the latter, ask yourself the following questions:

- Would you enjoy spending time with this person outside of work?
- Do you respect this person?
- Do you feel comfortable sharing your judgments with this person?
- Would you accept critical feedback from this person?

No one is a hundred percent objective, and we will all make judgements from time to time. Trusted and intimate associates will not reject us for our biases, but will respect and attempt to better understand where we are coming from, as we do for them. Likewise, when we are in healthy long-term business partnerships, we won't judge our partners for errant viewpoints.

Friends and Family

Like in business, the main challenge in relationships with family and friends is vulnerability. Most of us can acutely recall what it was like to be picked last for the dodgeball team. We remember when our entire class was invited to a party except for us. We wince recollecting how terrible it felt when we told our dad we wanted to become a professional ice skater and he retorted he would disown us if we did anything that stupid.

Our fear of rejection may be based on our experiences, but using this anxiety as the foundation of a relationship is a blueprint for problems. When we try to appeal to other people's standards to receive the affection we crave, we deviate from our authentic personality. In doing so, we lie to other people and to ourselves. We pretend we are superstar athletes, or we act as if we love party games, or we pursue extra biology classes instead of taking ice skating lessons.

Eventually, our real selves pop up and, if we have low self-esteem, we engage in diversions to avoid showing our true colors to prying friends and family. We may feign an injury on the dodgeball court. We may make up excuses for why we can't attend the party. We may surreptitiously spend our evenings skating on the ice pond. Since we are so entrenched in hiding who we are, many fail to consider how these types of actions might be getting them what they actually wanted. We are so immersed in our facade and the shame of our true selves we lose sight of our real selves.

Over time, when we step out from behind the curtain and onto the stage, at first the trust created in the relationship cracks. Your friends and family may feel rejected for not being worthy of your confidence and remove themselves from the relationship temporarily in order to process it. A lack of vulnerability upfront creates a fake relationship, which, when exposed, leads to hurt, pain, and anger.

Vulnerability leads to better connections. When we are vulnerable, we can be authentic. We can create connections that lead us to deeper parts of ourselves rather than away from ourselves. In giving ourselves permission to be who we are, we are more likely to give others permission for who they are, and will attract more Mercury Mind connections as a result. We might all hide a few small things from our families and friends, because it's not natural to share everything with everyone. But by hiding the fundamental pieces of our being, we do our family and friends a disservice. We aren't sharing our true selves. We're assuming we know how they will act toward us, and taking away the chance for them to do something different.

If we are vulnerable and we are rejected, maybe the relationship lacks the other elements necessary for a long-term, Mercury Mind connection. As painful as it may be, there is nothing wrong with not having a natural connection with someone you love. You can still love someone, support them, and maintain a solid relationship without having that unique spark that comes with a Mercury Mind Connection.

Remember we can have two authentic people who simply don't align. Even if you and your sister may be vulnerable and have high self-esteem, you may not connect. That's ok. Finding connections with family and friends is a three step process:

1. Become authentic with yourself
2. Find other authentic people

3. See whether those authentic people align with where you're at mentally and emotionally

If the relationship fails at Step Three, it wasn't meant to be. Part of authenticity and vulnerability is embracing and accepting the mystery of our Mercury Mind connections.

Romantic Relationships

The monumental challenge to true intimacy in romantic relationships is compartmentalization. We hyper-focus on specific aspects of our partner that we believe fulfill our needs, rather than embracing the person entirely. We do this through three mechanisms: fetishization, romanticization, and quid-pro-quo.

Fetishization

The first way we often compartmentalize our romantic relationships is through fetishization. When we fetishize, we remove intimacy and vulnerability and replace it with objectification. For example, we may hyper-focus on dating workaholic overachievers, neurotic artists, or sandy blonde American women. We often focus on these superficial qualities because we believe they embody a part of intimacy we want. Perhaps our dad was an overachiever and we want his approval. Or perhaps we want to be an artist so we date artists. Or maybe "the one who got away" was a sandy blonde American woman, so we're hoping to recreate that spark.

These preferences may be an outward manifestation of subconscious desires, but by concentrating on our fetishes instead of connecting with a person, we don't allow others to show us who they are. Moreover, we don't allow ourselves to be vulnerable.

Romanticization

Romanticization is an extension of fetishization. We write a script of who we want to be and the person we want to fulfill our desires. Typically, this person we've created doesn't exist, so we find a person who embodies most of these qualities and try to squeeze them into the mold of the person we'd like them to be.

When we obsess over this fantasy of a person, we don't allow our natural relationship to play out with them. We don't allow them to have their own thoughts, opinions, and faults. Moreover, we blind ourselves to who they are for the sake of clinging to our safe fantasy. Rather than giving both parties the grace to explore whether the relationship is a good fit, we make the declaration that we are an ideal match and do everything in our power to maintain the fantasy. When this illusion crumbles—as it always does—one or both parties is less connected to their true self.

It is important not to let our fear of vulnerability interfere with the natural process of connection. When we throw away the rigid rules, we find the potential for a deeper, more satisfying connection. Or we may find the relationship just isn't working, and give ourselves the freedom to let go so we can find a true Mercury Mind connection.

For example, maybe we staunchly hold on to the ideal of a man with good manners. So when our polite partner burps in our ear over the phone, we might react with disgust. How dare he be less than Mr. High Society! However, if we opened our mind to let this man be who he authentically is, we might give him the opportunity to show what the burp meant to him. Perhaps it wasn't a crude insult, but a compliment of how comfortable he feels together. Perhaps he felt like he didn't have to be buttoned-up all the time, and he could be real in our presence. By not allowing for this intimate moment, we shame him, forcing disconnection and favoring a fantasy image over real connection.

Quid-Pro-Quo

This type of romantic relationship is treated like a business transaction. You give me sex and I'll send you a text to show I'm thinking about you once in a while. You go to the basketball game with me, and I'll go shopping with you. You don't press your desires for marriage, and I'll come to dinner with your mom.

The problem with quid-pro-quo relationships is they are forged with compromises. Each compromise takes us further away from ourselves. As we make these subconscious deals and meld our Mercury Mind to someone else, the bond becomes toxic. When our partner bails on our vacation plans, we may question why they don't want to go out with us more often. We might spend hours googling ways to make them like us more. We might send vicious text messages blaming them for being selfish.

Even for the one who does most of the compromising in a quid-pro-quo relationship, that martyrdom does not lead to intimacy. Mercury may be attracted to other metals, but when it connects with another metal the mercury corrodes it. Even a heart of gold can dissolve in mercury. Likewise, although we might believe we are compromising out of generosity or love, we are poisoning ourselves by not allowing our partners to fully see us.

In a healthy relationship, both parties should be happy to be with each other and be able to openly and vulnerably discuss when they are not. The focus should be on strengthening the authentic connection with each other. This means each party brings who they are to the table and they both try to assess whether they genuinely enjoy being with each other. If they don't enjoy each other as is, or if they try to force each other to make sacrifices that pull them away from who they are, then the relationship ultimately won't work. Forcing it isn't the answer. Some connections simply aren't there.

Three Steps to Attracting Mercury Mind Connections

A Mercury Mind connection is the pot of gold at the end of the vulnerability rainbow.

Over time, toxic connections can erode us. Just as hatters who inhaled mercury fumes went mad, our minds corrode as we pull the wool over our own eyes. Eventually, we will be the ones conversing with teacups and Cheshire cats, delusional about who we are.

Alternatively, if we aim to authentically connect with others through deep relationships forged from our Mercury Minds, we can attach to other like people in the same way that mercury binds to itself. The objects and people we want to connect with are complex, and the only way to measure whether our relationships are built on a lasting connection is by allowing the space and time to cultivate true intimacy. We must build trust, care, and respect through thousands of small moments. We must allow the person to be flawed in their entirety and judge them not only on their green lights, but also on their neon flashing red ones. We should let our cycles stay open to the uncertain so we can learn more and let each other introduce ourselves over time. The relationship as a concept should never replace true intimacy.

There are three steps to connecting more deeply with ourselves and others. First we must understand our authentic values, so we can uncover our attractions and honest self. Then we can find ways to be okay with our attractions in order to develop a stronger sense of self-esteem. Finally, it's time to act on our attractions to see how they truly make us feel. The next three chapters outline this process in detail.

6

Step One, Identifying Our Attractions

Ask any group of people why they don't have love, happiness, and fulfillment in their lives and you'll get a laundry list of mostly predictable responses. They're lonely because they're not married. They're depressed because they're not famous actors. They're bored because they're not millionaires. We all think we know exactly what it would take to make our lives better, if only we could find a way to get those things.

However, this way of thinking is actually based on a misunderstanding of how attraction works. We define our life goals based on our *conscious* attractions, but often we don't actually want those things at all. What really makes us happy is becoming aware of our *subconscious* desires and learning to pursue those. But this is easier said than done. Our subconscious desires are buried deep down under layers of shame and guilt, and identifying them can be exceedingly difficult. Consider these three scenarios:

Zara aspires to become a criminal lawyer at a prestigious firm. After seven years of bone-grinding schoolwork, a $150,000 down payment for a brand-name law education, and four woefully underpaid associate and junior attorney positions, Zara finally lands a great job as a senior associate at her dream company. However, just three months into her new position, Zara develops crippling anxiety and the company fires her for incompetency. Now she's back to being unemployed, and her self-confidence is tanking.

Zach is forty pounds overweight. Each year, he vows on January 1 to get in better shape. He tells friends, family, and even his local grocer of his ambitions to hire a personal coach, switch to a vegetarian diet, and gear up to run the half-marathon in the fall. By January 31, however, he finds himself sacked out on the couch, game console in hand while guzzling ranch straight from the bottle. Come December, he finds himself sobbing disconsolately to the fat man in the mirror who's once again packed on ten additional pounds.

Zander is a professional surfer who claims his main goal in life is to find a great girl to settle down with. He believes if he had a serious relationship, he would feel satisfied with his life. Days, weeks, and months pass without a single date. Meanwhile, he spends most of his days catching waves on sun-soaked beaches and most of his nights burying his chagrin in tequila and a series of one-night stands with bikini models. He blames his lack of intimacy on the fact that he doesn't have a steady job, lacks a retirement account, and is only 5'7". The kind of women he's looking for always seem to go for the stable, tall, ambitious men.

The commonality between these anecdotes is each subject's goals do not align with their authentic desires. Zara tells herself she wants to be a high-powered criminal lawyer, but subconsciously she actually wants to pursue a less rigorous career path—maybe something more creative. Zach has set the conscious goal of getting in better shape, but he subconsciously wants to work as a tester for Blizzard Games. Zander, the surfer, is genuinely convinced that he will be happy when he finds the right girl to settle down with, but deep inside he wants to travel the world, surf epic swells, and bang beautiful women. These three people all think they are unhappy because they aren't getting what they want in life, but this isn't entirely true. In fact, the true problem is that their conscious and subconscious desires are in conflict. And, at the end of the day, their deeper drives are winning out.

Like mercury, we will always be magnetically drawn to fulfill our subconscious desires, which in the long term take precedence over the things we tell ourselves we want. Zara gets fired from her high-powered position, forcing her to do what she really wants and pursue a more artistic career. Zach stays on the couch all day improving his gaming chops so he can land the job he truly wants, testing games for Blizzard. Zander spends his days catching waves rather than looking for jobs on Wall Street because he really wants to travel the world and flirt with exotic cuties, not to meet someone serious and settle down. No matter how adamantly we tell ourselves that achieving our conscious goals will make us happy, we always end up moving toward our subconscious desires at the end of the day.

When there is a disconnect between our ambitions and our reality, this is often an indicator that what we think we want is not what we actually want. If we did actually desire something, we would not impose obstacles on our path to achieving it. If Zara truly wanted to be a lawyer, she would do whatever it takes to stay in her job. If Zach honestly desired a healthier body he would get his butt off the couch and into the gym. If Zander truly wanted to meet someone long term and settle down he'd move to a suburb and become a general manager at the local surf shop. When we aren't getting the things we tell ourselves we want, it's a sign that these conscious desires aren't in alignment with our more authentic attractions.

Zara, Zach, and Zander's unhappiness is not a result of not getting what they want. Their dissatisfaction lies in their inability to accept what they actually *do* want. They shame themselves and hoard resentment toward the outside world for preventing them from getting what they believe they desperately want. If instead, these three characters accepted what they subconsciously and authentically wanted, they would feel a sense of accomplishment instead of guilt. Furthermore, they would have the insight to direct themselves toward their authentic desires in a healthy way. Zara would happily quit her job and never look back. Zach would cancel his gym membership and stop feeling bad about his love handles. Zander would feel at peace with the fact that his nomadic bachelor lifestyle is exactly what he wants right now. Acceptance is the first brave step toward uncovering our subconscious authentic attractions.

Before we accept what we actually want, however, we must learn to unmask our true desires. And this isn't easy. Often, we believe if we accept our true desires, we won't like the person we become. Moreover, we will be rejected by others. If Zara quits her law job and becomes a painter, her father won't be proud of her anymore. If Zach embraces his pudge, his girlfriend will leave him. If Zander admits he only wants one night stands, his friends will think he's a player. Getting in touch with our true attractions is tough because it means making ourselves vulnerable to rejection from others.

The Roadmap to Authentic Living

The path to accepting our subconscious desires is a difficult one to walk. This journey requires us to become radically honest with ourselves about what we want, even if these revelations shatter our sense of self. We have to be willing to re-open cycles that we thought we closed for good long ago. The process involves stepping into the uncertain, disconnecting ourselves from our false perceptions of who we are, and embracing a more honest way of living. It can be a lonely journey, but it ultimately leads to deeper and more authentic connections with others.

If our authentic, subconscious wants are misaligned with our conscious wants, we feel a lingering sense of dissatisfaction. This dissatisfaction is merely inauthenticity by another name. The disconnection between what is real and what we consciously want to be true is what drives our inability to connect with our authentic selves. For instance, we might have a hard time accepting that we don't like sports, because we come from a family of die-hard football fans. But for as long as we continue to tell ourselves we can't wait to watch the big game we'll never feel truly in alignment with who we really are.

The trick to banishing our feelings of inauthenticity, dissatisfaction, and disappointment is discerning between our subconscious and conscious desires. When we can honestly see what our real wants are, we can embrace the reality of who we are and become the truest versions of ourselves, instead of a shell of the person we think we should be.

There are three main steps to this process.

Step 1 is identifying our true attractions, particularly the ones we do not want to accept. Before we can develop authentic mercury connections, we must understand which types of people, objects, and environments we are genuinely attracted to. To discover these subconscious wants, we can use specific physiological, mental, and situational indicators. Instead of labeling these attractions as good or bad, we must accept them without judgment as part of our mysterious Mercury Mind

Step 2 is to look deeper into our conscious attractions to explore what is driving them. Once we understand the societal and self-inflicted obstacles that prevent us from prioritizing our authentic desires, we can explore how our outwardly focused goals create toxicity in our lives. By asking continuous questions we can maintain a perpetual cycle of self-discovery, bringing our stated goals into closer alignment with our true wants.

Step 3 is to act on our authentic attractions without shame. By becoming more comfortable with what we honestly want, we will grow our self-esteem and open pathways to expressing our deepest desires in healthy, fulfilling ways. As we do this, we will foster more meaningful relationships, more intimate connections, and more purposeful living.

In this chapter, we will focus on Step 1.

The Danger of Not Accepting Our Authentic Attractions

Authenticity sounds nice, but is it really worth the discomfort and uncertainty of deeper self-exploration? Is it worth opening up all kinds of closed cycles and re-examining our basic assumptions about who we really are? If we relinquish our conscious ambitions of becoming an astronaut, chief executive, or superstar lover, what will we be left with? After all, most of us are accustomed to an undercurrent of dissatisfaction in our lives. For many, this discontent may even motivate us to achieve more than we thought we were capable of. Isn't it a good thing to set ambitious goals for ourselves? Don't we want to always be a little uncomfortable?

Despite what we might read in some of the popular self-help books, maintaining an illusion of superficial desires comes with dire consequences. The price of pandering to our facade is not merely a spoonful of disappointment when we don't reach our goals. It is not a "shoot for the moon and land among the stars" situation.

There are many mental and physical repercussions for living inauthentically, ranging from chronic stress to addictive behavior.

When there is a disconnect between our conscious and subconscious desires, we feel **distress**. This psychological state is a negative response to stressors in our lives, inciting feelings of anxiety, anger, and anguish. Distress arises out of our frustration; we gravitate toward our subconscious wants and away from our conscious desires, leaving us in a chronic state of disappointment for our failed attempts at achieving our desires.

Imagine someone who tells all his friends he wants to be a well-renowned screenwriter, but he subconsciously wants to be a stay-at-home dad. His conscious and subconscious desires are in conflict. Of course, those deeper, more authentic wants will tend to win out over time. He is much more likely to spend hours playing baseball with his son in the backyard than using the time to touch up the screenplay he's been working on for three years. There's nothing wrong with this. But he's going to feel bad about himself for not working harder toward his stated goals. Every hour he spends throwing the ball around will cause him more distress. Every time he watches a movie and sees the "screenplay by" credit roll across the screen his veins will flood with stress hormones. Despite the fact that this man is actually living in a relatively authentic way, he perceives himself to be a failure. So he feels distress constantly.

Distress also shows up when we *do* achieve our conscious desires, if doing so pulls us away from fulfilling our subconscious goals. For instance, our screenwriting dad might finish his masterpiece and sell a series to HBO. Now he has to live in Los Angeles for six months out of the year and he doesn't see his son for weeks at a time. He's achieved everything he told himself he wanted, but he still experiences the toxic feeling of distress because he is magnetized toward his subconscious desire to be an awesome stay-at-home dad. He is tortured with a feeling of deep dissatisfaction and he doesn't understand its genesis.

Simone Biles is another example of someone who achieved her conscious goals but still felt distress because she wasn't living in alignment with her deeper desires. Add to the list historic famous figures such as Van Gogh, Kurt Cobain, or even the beloved Robin Williams. Getting what we tell ourselves we want doesn't solve our problems. In fact, it can even lead us to feel more distressed as we move farther away from our authentic attractions.

When we experience distress, our bodies release cortisol in response. This stress hormone evolved as a temporary response to imminent danger. In the short term, it gives us the capacity for alertness, metabolism control, and inflammation regulation.[1] However, experiencing elevated cortisol levels on a chronic basis can also inhibit us. Persistently high levels of cortisol alter the immune system, suppressing reproductive health, physical growth, and digestive functions.[2] Moreover, cortisol has a strong correlation with accelerated biological aging[3], higher mortality, and chronic diseases such as diabetes and hypertension.[4]

There is also an inverted u-shaped relationship between cortisol levels and performance.[5] This means while moderate levels of cortisol might initially help with performance, high levels tend to inhibit our functioning in stressful situations, leading to clumsy and even catatonic responses. In other words, while we may believe our malcontent is motivating, the high level of cortisol associated with this state would indicate otherwise. Feeling bad about our lives doesn't push us to achieve greatness, it just makes us miserable.

The harsh reality is that distress is on the rise in modern society. On one hand, we have more lofty goals than ever before and we beat ourselves up for not being able to attain them. We see real people every day on social media with the mansion we want, the job we want, the husband we want, and the six-pack abs we used to have in college. So we tell ourselves we should have those things too, even if those goals are in conflict with our true authentic desires.

On the other hand, we have become better than ever at achieving our conscious goals. Thanks to the booming self-help industry and abundance of resources online from motivational gurus, it's easier than ever to bring our dreams to fruition. We really can get the job, body, car, or partner we've been telling ourselves we need. But once we do, we experience the Robin Williams effect. Our distress doesn't magically go away, it only magnifies.

This trend of distress is troubling. Studies show this painful emotional state explains why overall happiness is decreasing,[6] why there are rising rates of depressive and anxiety disorders,[7] and why there has been a drastic rise in chronic health conditions such as ischemic heart disease, diabetes, and kidney disease over the last thirty years, which amplified the devastation of the COVID-19 pandemic.[8] If we don't amend our approach soon, we will only succeed in killing ourselves faster, offsetting the substantial progress made by the last century of modern medicine.

Conversely, when we pursue our authentic attractions, we feel **eustress**. Unlike its vindictive older brother, eustress inspires feelings of hope, vigor, and inspiration. It is a positive stressor, rather than a negative one. We feel eustress in pursuing our authentic desires because we naturally gravitate toward fulfilling these wants. Without the interference of conflicting conscious desires, it is almost impossible for us not to achieve exactly what we want. When we inevitably fulfill these desires without the roadblocks, we are left feeling satisfied rather than disappointed.

Imagine a BMW-driving, hedge fund manager who wants to be a member of a premium country club. With his high income, golf prowess, and pink Ralph Lauren polo shirt, he is a shoo-in for membership. When he walks into the club for the first time, he feels the go-getter excitement of eustress. Now, if that man were trying to pursue a lifestyle that wasn't in accordance with his true self, he would feel distress. Say he tried to fit into a biker bar because his older brother told him it was cool. The other patrons would take one look at his pale blue shorts with the whales on them and kick him to the curb. He would feel humiliated, downtrodden, and defeated. Even if he swapped his golfer gear for a leather jacket and beat every biker in the Tri-state area at eight ball, he would still feel out of place. This hollow ambition would cause distress over time as he feels the weight of his unmet subconscious desires. By embracing that he is a luxury-seeking socialite, he trades "cool" for real and swaps dissatisfaction for positive ambition.

Preliminary data on eustress indicates that this state is associated with low-to-moderate cortisol levels and produces better performance than distress.[9] Some cortisol can be beneficial, and the low-to-moderate cortisol output of eustress puts us in the sweet spot to reap the advantages of this "stress hormone." Lower cortisol levels have been associated with higher psychological functioning[10] and eustress specifically correlates with better overall physical and mental health.[11] Moreover, people in a state of eustress are more amenable to positive feedback to help them achieve their goals.[12] Eustress motivates us rather than weighing us down.

The benefit of accepting our authentic attractions is not simply that doing so helps us to assuage feelings of discontent. Embracing our true desires is quite literally a matter of survival. When we accept and pursue what we honestly want deep down, we are healthier, happier, and live longer. But how can we distinguish between our subconscious and conscious desires?

Types of Attraction

Before we can delineate between our subconscious and conscious desires, it helps to understand exactly what attraction is and how it works. Often, we put feelings of comfort, sexual desire, and emotional longing together under the umbrella of attraction. However, not all of these feelings are controlled by the same internal processes.

Helen Fisher, renowned anthropologist, senior research fellow at The Kinsey Institute, and foremost expert on the biology of attraction proposed we have three independent brain systems for love and mating:[13]

1. Lust, which Fisher defines as the search for sexual gratification.
2. Attachment, which Fisher equates with companionate love.

3. Attraction, which Fisher equates with obsessive love and infatuation.

Fisher applied these systems primarily to classify mating relationships, but we can extend them to any kind of desire. We can lust after fame, obsess over mile-high luxury lofts, or feel attachment to our hometown church group. Our true, subconscious attractions are the type of desires that incite dominating thought patterns, hits of dopamine, and the sensation of butterflies. The attraction system leads to our greatest feelings of elation and our deepest feelings of despair. It is the root of both our happiness and unhappiness.

This distinction between these three systems is important because we tend to conflate sexual desire with both attraction and attachment. In fact, these systems are regulated by independent neurological networks. Lust is primarily regulated by hormones such as androgens and estrogen, associated with sexual arousal. Attachment is controlled primarily by the neuropeptides vasopressin and oxytocin, which engender feelings of companionship and connection. Attraction is controlled by dopamine, norepinephrine, and low levels of serotonin, which ignite excitement, passion, and those stomach butterflies that make us simultaneously want to swoon and puke.

Not only is the physiology different for each system, but the feelings each incites are distinct. Lust motivates us to seek out sexual union. Attachment makes us want to pursue comfort, security, and emotional connection. And attraction leads to intrusive thoughts and an obsessive need to connect with the object of our affection.

Fisher notes while these three systems often function in tandem, one does not necessarily beget the other. For example, men and women injected with androgens may have increased sex drive, but will not necessarily fall in love. This is important because a Mercury Mind connection is deeper than lust and distinct from attachment. It stems from the subconscious, uncontrollable, and obsessive feelings generated by the attraction system. This system is not only distinct on a theoretical level, but on a biological level.

When we approach attraction with this more focused definition, we can begin to parse out our true wants from the objects or people we lust after or feel attachment toward. Lust and attachment are our conscious wants. We feel lust toward objects that we think will give us immediate gratification. When we obtain something we've been lusting over, it can give us a small and superficial boost to our confidence. Similarly, we feel attachment toward people who have historically provided us with feelings of familiarity and certainty. Indulging our desire for attachment makes us feel safe and assuages our fear of uncertainty. This can help us close some of those open cycles. True attraction, on the other hand, isn't so safe. And it doesn't give us a quick confidence boost. When we pursue our deepest desires we might feel uncertain and there is no guarantee of satisfaction. Yet, the pursuit of this type of authentic attraction is the only thing that will connect us with our true selves.

Imagine a construction worker who lusts after dark-skinned beauties, but is attached to his high school sweetheart. If he has an affair with a Sri Lankan woman, he may feel temporary satiation. If he stays faithful to his cornfed, milk-skinned wife, he may feel comfortable. However, both options will leave him feeling unsatisfied because they are temporary solutions. What he honestly desires might be something else entirely.

The women may simply be an indicator of the construction worker's deeper wants: security, connection, and a satisfying sexual life all in one. If he does not accept his attractions, he will continue to harbor growing feelings of dissatisfaction and eventually find unhealthy ways to pursue his desires. By acknowledging his true attractions, he opens himself up to pursue what he actually wants in a healthy way. Perhaps this means role playing with his wife, or asking for a divorce, or simply seeking a more sexually intimate relationship with himself. The possibilities for solutions are endless if only he permits himself the grace of acceptance.

How to Identify Our True Attractions

There are three primary indicators of true attraction: 1) Physiological and neurological indicators, 2) Distress and eustress, and 3) Situational indicators.

Physiological and Neurological Indicators

While it's not exactly practical to monitor our internal processes by measuring the levels of our neurotransmitters, it is possible to look at some physiological indicators to help us delineate between conscious wants and true attractions. For example, dopamine is correlated with vigilance, pursuit of goals, and feelings of reward. When we take a hit of cocaine, which gives us a jolt of dopamine, we feel a huge burst of energy, positivity, and excitement.[14] Norepinephrine increases our heart rate, incites anger, and stimulates our "fight or flight" reflex.[15] It can make us hyper-focused on a potential relationship, obsessing about winning over a certain individual. Low levels of serotonin are correlated with feelings of romantic love.[16] Curiously, since serotonin is the "happiness hormone," which regulates our mood and feelings of well-being, low levels can correlate with depression and anxiety.[17] Fluctuating serotonin levels can cause us to feel on top of the world in one moment, and buried under a torrential pile of shit in the next. Serotonin can also impact our appetite and sleep, which is often why people who are falling deeply in love can hardly keep down a french fry and might sleep only four hours a night.

While all of these physiological indicators might seem like a lot to ingest, here are some physiologically-related questions you can ask yourself to determine whether you feel a true attraction toward something:

- What takes your breath away?
- What makes your palms sweat?
- What gets your blood pumping?
- What makes you feel the proverbial butterflies in your stomach?
- What do you obsess over?
- What do you hyper-focus on?
- What do you find yourself working toward?
- What do you want to run away from?
- What makes you angry?
- What makes you the happiest you've ever been?
- What makes you the saddest you've ever been?

- What do you think about most of the day?

By answering these questions, we can begin to see the fumes of the intoxicating vapor of attraction we are all consumed by. This true attraction is nearly always at the forefront of our mind, yet many of us refuse to acknowledge its existence. By following the physiological and mental indicators of our obsessions, we can begin to unveil our true attractions.

Imagine, for example, we find ourselves obsessing every day about our terrible experience in school. We tell people we will never, ever go back to higher education, even if someone paid us a million dollars. Even though we have graduated, our thoughts keep returning to our daily experiences there five years later. While we might, therefore, conclude we hated school, this obsession may actually be an indicator we are attracted to the further pursuit of education. The mental energy we invest in thinking about school indicates despite our painful experience, there is a part of the school experience we are insatiably drawn to. It may not be school itself, but there is a deep attraction to the experience that relentlessly pulls us in. The more we resist this attraction, telling ourselves that we hate school, the more we solidify it. No matter how the movies paint it, attraction is not always wrapped up in a pretty bow tied, around Hugh Jackman or Selma Hayeck. Attraction can be what we fear the most.

If after going through these physiological indicators you still feel unsure whether a specific desire bears the markers of Mercury Mind attraction, ask yourself one final question: Are you trying to talk yourself into it, or are you trying to talk yourself out of it? If you are trying yourself into it, then chances are you're not genuinely attracted to it. In those cases, it is best to leave it be. If you're trying to talk yourself out of it, chances are you are magnetized to it. It promises those highs, yet the consequences of failure may make you feel like running. That is serotonin at its best.

Distress and Eustress

The feelings of distress and eustress are controlled by different physiological systems than attraction, and they signify slightly different things. While the physiological indicators of the attraction system signify whether or not we are truly drawn to something, feelings of distress and eustress indicate the fulfillment or non-fulfillment of those attractions.

When assessing whether a desire is a genuine attraction or not, we can look at how the pursuit and attainment of this desire would feel to us. Distress is associated with negative feelings in response to stressors, while eustress is a positive response to stress.

Our subconscious, genuine attractions can incite both distress and eustress. When we are not authentically pursuing our true desires, we feel distress. When we are in active pursuit of our genuine wants, we feel eustress.

To determine whether an attraction ignites distress or eustress, we simply have to ask whether pursuing that desire feels exciting or foreboding. If we enjoy the pursuit, the desire is most likely genuine. If we are struggling to feel positive, we are most likely pursuing a superficial conscious desire and neglecting our deeper subconscious attractions. More telling, if we achieve the object of our desire and our feelings of positivity dissipate and are replaced with indicators of distress, then we have most likely attained a conscious want, which provided us with a temporary hit of satisfaction, but did not satiate a true attraction.

For example, I collect sports cars. I genuinely enjoy the elements of speed, style, and engineering that come together to maximize the performance of these cars. When I am hunting for a new car, I enjoy the investigation and the pursuit. I would drive a performance car if I was the only person left on Earth. That is simply how much I love this type of car.

However, imagine instead if I was the kind of person who wanted to fill a void in my life with this type of vehicle. I would feel anxiety and distress, wondering whether I could navigate life without such vehicles. Or maybe I'd be excited at first but then, once I got the new car, I might quickly feel disappointment, anger, and resentment set in if the vehicle didn't immediately get me the attention desired.

Situational Indicators

If you are not where you want to be and don't feel good about where you are, it is likely you are facing a disconnect between your conscious and subconscious desires. We naturally gravitate toward our conscious desires, so if we tell ourselves we want to obtain a certain object, goal, or person, yet don't take steps to actually pursue that attraction, it is an indication that what we say we want is not what we truly want.

Compare the violin virtuoso to the office worker who keeps telling her friends she wants to pick up the fiddle again, but never finds the time. The virtuoso returns to the violin day and night without fail. She treats it like a lover. She revels in her time with it. When she is away from home, she thinks about playing. The office worker never gets around to practicing. Her fiddle sits collecting dust in the corner of her closet. Occasionally, she'll take a peek at the peeling case, yet her mind will quickly wander to other pursuits. She does not genuinely want to pick up the fiddle again, no matter how she brags to friends that she could have been a folk rock superstar in another life.

If we keep returning to our objects of affection, then we are genuinely attracted to them. If we feel great about who we are, where we are in our lives, and what we're investing our time in, then we're likely pursuing our true attractions. Even if we haven't attained the object of our desires, if we are enjoying the journey, it is a simple, yet meaningful indication we are on a genuine path toward our true deep inner goals.

Acceptance of Attractions

When we can see our attractions in all their naked glory, we have the opportunity to accept or deny them. Denial is damaging. When we accept our attractions, we can view them as positive challenges rather than negative obstacles. While this initial acceptance is difficult, the rewards of eustress, authenticity, and a real shot of satisfaction are worth the discomfort of ripping the bandaid off the bullet wound and exposing our blood, tendons, and bone for the world to see.

Is the uninhibited acceptance of our attractions really advisable, given some desires might lead to unhealthy habits? Imagine we are authentically attracted to spending our days in a heroin den. This is not the safest place to hang out for the afternoon. However, in cases where we find seemingly true desires that cause us pain, it is often an indication we need to look deeper into our attractions. Maybe we are drawn into the heroin den because we're seeking connection, comfort, and community. This attraction is real, yet the problem and pain lies not in the attraction, but in our method of pursuing it.

If we were to admit we wanted connection, comfort, and community, then we could open ourselves to all of the ways we may fulfill those genuine desires.

In her audiobook "Kick Ass", motivational coach, Ted Talk speaker, and bestselling author of "The 5 Second Rule," Mel Robbins includes several one-on-one coaching sessions with her clients. In session six, one of those clients, Jesse, laments that at 5'7 and 293 pounds, she has spent most of her life struggling to lose weight. She describes herself as being uncomfortable in her own skin and afraid to be seen.

In homage to Robbins' expertise, she quickly dismantles Jesse's story.

"I think," Robbins says, "You're pissed off when you're not the center of attention."

Robbins points out how Jesse actually likes being in front of people. Her weight makes her presence undeniable whenever she walks into a room. She can use her huge body to take up space, make people see her, and intimidate others into doing what she wants (like getting her husband to do chores). Robbins says Jesse has no intention or desire to lose weight because it would take away her power.

Since Jesse hasn't taken any action to lose weight in the last decade, it is easy to see losing weight is not a true attraction for her. However, as Robbins highlights, Jesse's true attraction is to power.

While Jesse's method of achieving empowerment is unhealthy, her desire for attention is genuine and therefore should not be condemned. The solution is not to change her attraction to feeling powerful, but to redirect the way in which she pursues this attraction.

When we condemn our attractions we can fall into a pattern of shaming ourselves. This wreaks havoc on our self-esteem and forces us to pursue false attractions. Ultimately, we will be ever-drawn back into our initial attraction and left feeling disappointed, hurt, and angry with ourselves. It's not the attraction itself that is the problem, it's pursuing our desires in unhealthy ways that gets us into trouble.

The only path forward is through relentless acceptance of our true attractions, even if we dislike the package they are wrapped in. We know we are in an unhealthy cycle when our mind and heart are at war, and our heart continues to win the battles even though it makes us hurt. In those cases, the answer is not to throw the heart in iron shackles, but to accept it for what it is. When we consciously accept our heart's true desires, we open a pathway for our mind to work with our heart to find alternative solutions to pursue our authentic desires. This collaboration opens the road to healthy attractions.

However, there are many roadblocks on the way to accepting our true attractions. We must find a shameless path to pursuing our attractions in the face of societal and internal barriers.

7

Step Two, Releasing Our Conscious Attractions

"I could have done it, father!" Loki screams, "I could have done it. For you. For all of us."

"No, Loki," Odin whispers.

Loki releases his grip on the hammer and falls, hand outstretched, into the abyss, realizing he's made an unredeemable mistake.

Loki, the villain of the 2011 Marvel movie *Thor*, struggles with a misalignment between his conscious and subconscious desires. On the surface he wants to dominate others, and this leads him to deceive people in pursuit of power. However, on a deeper level he is desperate to win the acceptance of his adoptive father, Odin. Ironically, the actions Loki takes in an attempt to fulfill his conscious desire end up moving him farther away from getting what he really wants.

This inner conflict comes to a head when Loki discovers his biological father, Laufey, is Odin's enemy. When Loki realizes this disparity between who he is and who he wants to be, he reacts by leaning into his conscious desire for control. He believes dominating others is the quickest pathway to winning Odin's respect.

If only I can conquer the Frost Giants by myself, Loki thinks, *then I will be worthy of my father's love.* Although there is nothing inherently wrong with Loki's desire for Odin's regard, the actions he chooses set off a chain reaction of devastating events, fracturing his relationships and ultimately dismantling the security of multiple worlds. When his attempts to win Loki's love through domination backfire, he doubles down on this conscious desire rather than letting it go. Ultimately, Loki turns his domination tendencies on Odin, even going as far as taking his adoptive father hostage.

By allowing his conscious desire for power to direct his actions, Loki alienates himself from the respect he so desperately wants. The more Loki vies for power, the less Odin approves of him. This creates internal conflict and a feeling of disconnection. As Loki pursues his conscious plan, he moves away from his true self.

While few of us might identify with the struggles of a Marvel supervillain, most can find Loki's inner conflict relatable. Loki suffers from a misalignment between his conscious and subconscious desires. And he becomes so attached to the conscious goal that he can't let go, even when it's preventing him from getting what he truly wants at his core. This is a common human problem. Many of us, in an attempt to fulfill our authentic desires, commit ourselves to a conscious goal that takes us farther from our true selves.

While the first step to shamelessly living as our true selves was to recognize our subconscious desires, the second step is to stop getting in our own way. When we let go of the conscious goals that are holding us back, we can free ourselves to directly pursue our authentic wants.

How Conscious Desires Hold Us Back

The actions we take to pursue our conscious goals will often fail to bring us closer to our subconscious core desires. When this happens we have a choice to make. We can shift our conscious desires, trying out a new strategy to get what we authentically want. Or we can dig our heels in deeper and commit to our old plan with new vigor. As we move through life we are constantly coming to these forks in the road and choosing whether to recommit to our conscious goal or allow ourselves to develop a new one.

Sometimes we decide to change our surface level desires. For instance, a skinny video gamer, tired of striking out with the ladies, might suddenly decide to start lifting weights and guzzling protein shakes. Other times, however, we double down on our strategies. The same gamer might decide he doesn't really want a girlfriend anyways, and recommit to his goal of beating *Final Fantasy V* in under twelve hours.

Both of these paths, recommitment or reassessment, are examples of forcing a cycle closed rather than allowing it to naturally close itself. When we double down on our conscious plans we are refusing to reopen the cycle at all. Similarly, when we change our conscious goals, we reopen the cycle and force it closed again. Either way, we move farther away from what we authentically want.

However, there is a third option. If we can detach ourselves from our conscious desires, and let them go, we can remain true to ourselves. We can keep the cycle open and allow it to reach a natural resolution.

Sixteen-year-old Marcie authentically craves her father's approval, so she announces she wants to be a factory floor supervisor when she grows up, just like her dad. Her father, however, poo-poos this idea. Girls don't work in factories with machinery. At this point, Marcie could go in one of two directions. She could employ the Loki strategy of doubling-down on her conscious desire, working to become the best floor supervisor in the industry, to hell with what her dad thinks. Alternatively, Marcie could let go of the supervisor idea and try something else to win dad's love, like ballet.

With either strategy, Marcie progressively distances herself from her authentic desire. If she pursues bulldozer glory, her traditional father may deepen his enmity over the fact that his daughter doesn't conform to traditional gender stereotypes. But if Marcie trades the factory for tutus, she may feel like she is moving further from her true self, deteriorating her self-esteem and fostering resentment toward her father. Both options involve closing the cycle as quickly as possible. But does a sixteen-year-old really need to commit to a life plan? Could she leave the cycle open?

If Marcie could let go of her conscious desire to settle on a father-approved career path, she might naturally discover another pathway to the love she authentically wants. Instead of deciding on a life trajectory as a teen, she might wait until age twenty-three, when she discovers her passion for holistic medicine and wins admiration from her dad for doing something she is truly inspired about.

Committing to a conscious desire, particularly a long-term one, closes our cycles and allows us to escape the feelings of uncertainty that arise from being unattached to a definite plan. Forcing our cycles closed with a conscious plan helps buffer the anxiety of uncertainty. Keeping a cycle open, however, requires a very healthy sense of inner worth. For instance, Marcie had to wait seven years to finally close the cycle and earn her father's respect—that's not easy.

The Need For Acceptance

As a social species, humans naturally seek acceptance from our peers. Our ancestors needed each other to survive. Without help from our tribe, we could not raise a helpless infant, gather food, protect ourselves from invaders, and kill the antelope on the plain for dinner. If we were banished from our community, the risk of mortality was high. In industrialized countries today, we experience a greater measure of individualism than our Paleolithic ancestors could ever have dreamed of. We can have Whole Foods deliver food to our front door. We can earn a living with nothing more than a laptop. We can even conceive a child with just a $1,000 deposit at a local sperm bank and a turkey baster.[1]

Despite these technological advances, however, the vestiges of our ancestral habits still live in us. Our mating choices, learning techniques, and cultural identity are all rooted in our desire for acceptance by our community. In fact, decades of research consistently shows that, despite our capacity for individual functioning, we experience significant mental and physical repercussions when we are socially isolated.[2] For example, during the COVID-19 lockdowns rates of depression, anxiety, and cardiovascular disease increased significantly.[3][4]

Being ousted from our communities elicits a neurological response that mimics physical pain.[5] This torture of rejection can lead to extreme reactions. It is why the sole liberal in a conservative town will sink into misanthropic hermitage, the LGBTQ kid from Louisiana will cut off all ties with her Baptist family, and the student who was bullied for ten years shows up to school with her father's rifle. Rejection is painful and, in some heartbreaking cases, deadly.

As a result of the dire mental and physical consequences from a lack of acceptance, many people opt to adapt their behavior to be more appealing to their community. Following the group activates the same part of our brain as receiving a reward.[6] Consequently, every time we conform to group behavior we receive a little hit of happy hormones. Even if these conforming behaviors, beliefs, or desires can be unhealthy for us as individuals, our brain essentially tells us "Good job!" every time we go with the group and gain acceptance.

In fact, as humans there is substantial evidence to show we actively reject facts that don't align with the worldview of our community.[7] This is called "motivated reasoning," and it actually gets more intense at increased educational levels, not less.[8] A 2015 metastudy on climate change revealed that the ideological divide widens with increasing knowledge of politics, science, and energy. In other words, the more information we collect, the more we are able to rationalize our existing beliefs, and the beliefs of the group to which we want to belong.

This pattern of reinterpreting any incoming information to bolster our existing viewpoints can also apply to desires. As we gain more information, we use it to further justify our superficial wants. For example, a woman who wants to be a millionaire entrepreneur might experience a massive panic attack every time she tries to close a new deal. Instead of using this information to question whether she actually wants this life, she doubles down. She tells herself the anxiety means she really cares about her job.

As we age, we gain more information about the world. But we don't grow more open-minded as a result. Actually, we tend to become further cemented in the identity we've adopted to appeal to our immediate communities. We gradually transition further away from our authentic desires and toward more socially acceptable goals for our lives as we endure the small cuts and gaping wounds of social rejection. By adopting acceptable goals and using any additional information we collect as confirmation that we are doing the right thing, we can avoid the pain of ostracism.

For example, the man who swore at fifteen he'd never work in a cubicle finds himself at forty-five, in a law office for sixty hours a week to support his wife and three kids. Over the years, the culture drilled into him that a man must provide financially for his family. Instead of questioning this, he gradually conformed and convinced himself that he actually kind of likes working so hard. He tells himself he's surely doing the right thing.

Similarly, the animal lover might find herself working in a lab that dissects mice for cancer research. Her family prioritizes job security and, when she was rejected from veterinary school, they convinced her to take the research position. Wanting to be a good daughter, she rationalized her career by telling herself she's doing it in the name of science. Actually, her work may even help non-human creatures one day.

The same phenomenon is at play with the peace-loving hippy who gradually becomes a war-mongering boomer as his friends age out of orgies and into social security checks. Tired of staying quiet at the weekly poker game when the guys all complain about "the damn foreigners stealing our jobs," he relinquishes his liberal viewpoint in favor of friendship. He now justifies war as necessary to protect the interests of his country.

As we grow up, consistent rejection and challenges to our true attractions deteriorate our self-esteem. As our self-esteem erodes, our need to prove we are worthy of acceptance supersedes our need to fill our authentic desires. This need becomes immediate as our survival instincts kick in and the little voice inside whispers that if we don't marry the surgeon, or land the job with a 401k, or buy a house in the right neighborhood, we will be ousted from our communities and forced to fend for ourselves. Then, we'll die.

Of course, our survival instincts aren't rooted in reality. We won't actually die if we don't conform. But it sure feels this way. The grand lie we tell ourselves is that we must conform to gain acceptance, be worthy, and get what we want. The problem with this line of thinking is that acceptance derived from an inauthentic compromise is always temporary. The more we commit to conscious desires to close our cycles and avoid rejection, the less authentic we become. The ultimate result is an erosion of our self-esteem.

The irony is the conscious desires we adopt to bolster our confidence actually *contribute* to our deteriorating self-worth. Our subconscious feelings of shame over what we perceive to be socially unacceptable authentic desires erodes our self-concept.

The ex-hippy might continually feel at odds with his friends' disregard for human life. However, he knows he would be judged as 'weak' for preferring a peaceful resolution over a violent insurrection, so he develops conscious desires that help him to cope. Maybe he keeps company with a bottle of Jack. This desire to drink himself numb turns into a nightly phenomenon. He cannot escape his need for approval, and yet his behavior is pulling him further away from himself, so he develops a new desire to escape all together.

The Origins of Unhealthy Desires

No authentic desire is inherently unhealthy. Genuine wants are not good, bad, harmful, or helpful. They simply are. And they are *simple*. Food, shelter, belonging, comfort, respect, love, and purpose are all examples of authentic cravings. These types of genuine desires are rooted in basic human needs. They are rudimentary essentials, established during our youth, that we spend our lives striving to achieve.

Our conscious desires, on the other hand, often deflect, mask, restrict, and minimize our genuine wants. For instance, we might have a conscious goal of getting high. Maybe on some level we believe this will help us gain a sense of connection with others. Or perhaps we use the drug to distract ourselves from the fact that we feel alone and disconnected. Either way, there is nothing wrong with having a genuine want to connect with others. The problem is with the conscious desire we are focusing on, not the authentic goal underneath it.

A conscious attraction is usually either something we subconsciously think is related to a true attraction, or else it is a way of numbing the pain we feel at not obtaining a true attraction. Both types of conscious attractions can lead to unhealthy patterns because they are not tethered to who we genuinely are.

Sue is a biomedical engineering student with a genuine desire for a romantic partner she connects with deeply. However, after being mocked by her sorority sisters for 'desperately' wanting a boyfriend, she subconsciously concludes she needs to adjust her strategy to be accepted by her friend group. As a compromise, Sue objectifies men with her peers and revels in fleeting companionship through a series of one-night stands. Soon enough, Sue's player strategy becomes interwoven into her external identity, even though it is not in alignment with her true wants. Unchecked, this leads Sue to devalue men. As she grows older and her friends get into long-term relationships of their own, Sue's attachment to this strategy could alienate her from both her friends and the men she dates, who tire of her superficial connections. In the long term, this attachment to being a player can lead her away from her genuine desire to connect with her friends and with a partner. We must be aware of third party influences that are not in alignment with our Mercury Mind.

Alternatively, Sue could use her 'player' status to distract herself from the fact that she isn't obtaining her true desire. Maybe what Sue truly wants is a romantic connection with another woman, but she can't admit this to her friends or to herself. She believes by having sex with lots of men she can make herself into the straight woman her friends will accept. In this case, Sue is playing out a psychological phenomenon known as reaction formation, whereby we adopt a conscious desire that is the opposite of our true wants, to protect us from the ridicule we may incur from revealing our authentic selves. The problem with this strategy is that we cannot escape our true desires, and we end up grasping for increasingly extreme measures to bury our subconscious impulses. Eventually, we will no longer be able to contain them.

As Sue's shame over her true desires increases, her self-esteem will decline, and she might bury herself deeper under a pile of increasingly riskier and more damaging strategies. Maybe she sees her female friends in the shower, then goes out to a party and hooks up with three different men. Or perhaps she develops feelings for a female coworker, and then gets engaged to the man she's been casually dating. Soon enough, Sue is propositioning women in the bathroom while doubling as a homemaker and advocating against gay marriage.

Anytime we try to focus on our conscious desires rather than our genuine wants, we are prematurely closing a cycle. Often, we do not possess the breadth of understanding to be able to meet our genuine wants through making a conscious plan. In this case, the key is to step back from our surface level desires and get in touch with what we honestly crave.

Regardless of how hard we try to control others' perceptions of us, the truth is that people like us better when we are in touch with our genuine selves. Humans are naturally drawn toward authenticity. We admire people like Nelson Mandela, Oscar Wilde, and Pablo Picasso because they embrace the hard truths about themselves, and don't attempt to hide in order to please society.

We love authenticity in other people, so why wouldn't other people prefer this quality in us too? In fact, "being yourself" in relationships is correlated with secure attachment, more successful long-term partnerships, and deeper connections with individuals similar to our genuine selves.[9] Authenticity leads to Mercury Mind connections.

Ironically, we don't gain true acceptance by perverting our authentic desires. Enduring connections don't come when we give in to conscious desires that are more common. Rather, they arise when we embrace who we are and what we genuinely want. Fully accepting our true selves will ultimately lead to more profound acceptance from others.

This self-reliance builds our self-esteem, even in the face of uncertainty. We may not be able to direct how our authentic desires play out through conscious wants, but through a solid sense of self we can begin to see the full scope of what is possible. We can take advantage of the many opportunities all around us to fulfill our authentic desires.

If Sue were to accept her desire for a romantic relationship with a woman, she may very well lose friends. But then she can take the job opportunity in San Francisco and make friends in her new city who see her for the person she genuinely is. She can say "no" to the attractive man asking her to the movies. She can accept the invitation to go out for drinks with her attractive female coworker. Once Sue gets in touch with her genuine desires, her actions can stem from a more authentic place. She will no longer feel the need to hide who she is in order to fit in. And this will ultimately lead her to find more meaningful connections with new friends and lovers, even if it means losing her old friends at first. Plus, she will feel better about herself when she is able to get comfortable with who she really is, and will be able to keep her cycles open and handle the uncertainty of forging a new path in life.

The same goes for all of us. We are all clinging to some conscious goals that aren't serving us. When we can let those go and embrace our deeper desires we will begin to live more authentically. We might face some rejection at first, but ultimately, we will find more meaningful connections as we develop a more profound knowledge of who we really are. But how do we separate our conscious wants from our authentic attractions?

Distinguishing Our Desires

Often, shame leads us to deny our authentic attractions. The first step in detangling our conscious wants from our authentic desires is to get brutally honest about which behaviors in our lives are causing us pain. We start by admitting that we have a problem. This process is similar to attending your first Alcoholics Anonymous meeting. Like an alcoholic, we all have conscious wants that are unhealthy. We can't change until we get honest about these.

"Hi, my name is Aurora and I'm an alcoholic."

Or… "I'm addicted to buying thousand-dollar pairs of shoes even though I wipe out my bank account for each shopping trip."

Or… "I have an insatiable knack for getting into emotionally abusive relationships with narcissistic bad boys."

Or… "I keep pursuing jobs that make me want to burn the building down every time I'm on break."

We all have unhealthy patterns born from harmful superficial desires. When we can admit these hurtful wants and talk about the person they have made us become, we can see who we are meant to be. There is a person with genuine wants buried underneath the alcoholic who drowns in a 12-pack of Budweiser or 3 bottles of wine each night.

The more we become aware of our true wants, buried beneath the conscious desires we have tethered our identity to, the more we can accept our genuine selves. We know we have found an authentic desire when we get down to something undeniably simple. Do you want safety, companionship, or respect? If we have an insatiable craving for a rum and coke, we might actually want to feel good about ourselves. When we are drawn to an abusive partner, we might really desire protection. When we pursue jobs that make us miserable, maybe our underlying desire is simply financial security. Beneath our unhealthy conscious attractions are simple wants.

Repeat this process of rabbit hole questioning, digging deeper until you reach the level where your desires are neither good nor bad, but simply and irrevocably human.

Goal-Setting From Our True Desires

Once we dig deep enough to identify an authentic attraction, we can transition from awareness to acceptance. Often our subconscious desires are shrouded in shame. On some level we are afraid others won't approve of our true wants, so we judge our attractions as bad. This leads us to internalize a sense of shame. Healing from this shame is how we build authentic self-esteem. Loki simply wants Odin's respect. But he is scared of being judged if he admits this to himself or others. If he could get over this shame he might be able to seek respect through a different avenue other than domination. For example, his brother, Thor, offered to collaborate on numerous missions, but Loki repeatedly turned these invitations down. Accepting one of these offers may have given Loki the feeling of respect he craved.

Conscious desires are not necessarily bad. However, they should always be directly serving our authentic subconscious attractions. Problems arise when we grow attached to a conscious desire and are unable to let it go, even when it is clearly no longer serving us or when it becomes obvious that it's unhealthy for us in the long-term.

Jeannie's authentic desire is to be recognized as an important member of her community. As a child, she was lauded for her ability to play the organ, so she aspired to become the Sunday service organist at her local church. However, with age, she developed arthritis, making playing each week a painful endeavor. While her conscious desire to play the organ served her authentic attraction to connect with her community for many years, it is now becoming unhealthy. If she clings to this conscious desire, she may force herself to continue with an activity that brings her substantial pain. This could eventually cause Jeannie to become irritable, sabotaging her authentic desire to connect with her community.

If instead Jeannie recognizes her authentic desire and accepts that connection is what she really wants, she can let this painful activity go and find other ways to connect with members of her community. She could volunteer, teach music, lead the choir, or bake cookies! The possibilities are endless if she can act from a place of inner truth.

At any moment, most of us have multiple conscious and subconscious attractions at play. Though it may sometimes feel as though these goals are in conflict, there are always many ways we can fulfill our desires—even if we are unable to see these options in the present. Instead of trying to resolve the conflicts and immediately decide on a plan of action, a better answer is to leave our cycles open. We can trust that methods for fulfilling our genuine desires will present themselves throughout our lives in surprising ways, if only we have patience.

Charles genuinely wants to find a loving relationship with a woman, but he also desires financial security, which he believes he must obtain before he develops a long-term relationship. However, Charles works a minimum wage job at a RadioShack and, without a college degree, his prospects for financial security in the near future are limited. Since he needs more money to support a successful relationship, his desires seem to be in conflict. However, if he were to step back, he may see how the two goals can co-exist. He could pursue a loving relationship with someone who wants to support him as he attends night school and transitions to a more lucrative career. Or he might meet someone who has a great job and wants him to be a stay-at-home father. Or he could find a partner who doesn't care about money at all.

Once we can begin to act from our true desires and cultivate the patience to leave our cycles open, pathways to fulfilling those desires will present themselves. Our conscious goals may change if we find they are not in alignment with our true wants, and that's ok. We can always use our authentic desires as a barometer to test whether our goals are in alignment.

If Sandra's genuine desire is to buy a home, her conscious goal might be to land the highest paying job she can find. However, instead of running off to apply for investment banking positions that don't inspire her, she could leave her cycle open and she might find unexpected success through the creative knitting projects she sells at the local craft market. While a high-paying Wall Street position might get her into a new home faster than her yarn creations, the artistic endeavor brings her genuine joy.

When We Accept Ourselves, Our Attractions May Change

When we get more comfortable with our true desires we build self-esteem, and our attractions may morph as a result. For example, as you accept all aspects of yourself, you may find your need for admiration from others fades away. When this type of shift happens, it's ok to let go. Be vulnerable enough to allow your attractions to change as you do.

The process of reevaluating who we are and what we want, and accepting those truths, is not a one-time endeavor. It is an ongoing journey. After a lifetime of focusing on our conscious desires, it can be challenging to adopt this mindset and openness. However, it becomes easier the more we practice accepting ourselves. The more comfortable we become with our authentic desires, the more our self-esteem will grow. Eventually we may find we only truly need acceptance from one person: the one in the mirror.

When we can fully accept our authentic desires, it's time to explore them…

8

Step Three, Embracing Our True Attractions

Standing before hundreds of graduating students at the Maharishi International University in Iowa, actor Jim Carrey offered a sincere wish for every member of the audience, "I just want you to relax and dream up a good life."

These simple words carry a hard truth. Freeing ourselves from our self-imposed stresses is an essential part of getting what we want. Letting go allows us to dream, which gives us the opportunity to pursue our authentic desires.

During the speech, Carrey recounted the story of his father, who chose the safe career path of being an accountant over the unstable life of trying to make it as a comedian.[1] When Carrey was twelve, however, his father lost his 'safe' job, hurtling the family into abject poverty. There is no guarantee with anything in our lives, Carrey pointed out, so when we choose an inauthentic path because we believe it will be safer, we are fooling ourselves. We are closing the cycle and tricking ourselves into thinking we have nothing to worry about. But our cycles can always open back up again when we least expect them to. Carrey argued it is better to ask the universe for what we actually want than to spend our lives trying to avoid failure.

"You could spend your whole life imagining ghosts, worrying

about the pathway to the future," said Carrey with his characteristic Ace Ventura grin, "but all there will ever be is what's happening here in the decisions we make in this moment, which are happening here; which are based in either love or fear. So many of us choose our path out of fear disguised as practicality."

Carrey's words highlight the importance of letting go. He says we can't get what we truly want until we release the socially approved avatars we've constructed for ourselves, the compromises we've made to keep our heads above water, and the conscious goals we've adopted to squeeze ourselves into the safe little crannies of society. To attain our deepest desires, we must be willing to release ourselves out into the world in our rawest form. To show up for what we authentically want, we can't be focused on what other people want for us.

The issue Carrey is speaking of also shows up in the workplace, where it was recently dubbed 'The Great Resignation.' During the COVID-19 pandemic, a whopping 20% of U.S. workers switched careers and nearly half considered a job shift.[2] Even as the worst of the Coronavirus faded away, the number of employees leaving their jobs reached an all-time high of 4.5 million in November 2021.[3] This monumental shift will impact our economy for years to come.

Many journalists harbor immovable opinions on the causes of this trend—the indolent nature of Millennial employees, the inequitable pay structure of corporate America, or the pandemic's upheaval of our emotional, societal, economical structure, which led us to reevaluate how we spend our time. However, these beliefs miss an important component of this mass exodus. This "great resignation" is a reaction to uncertainty. Like Jim Carrey's father, people realized the conventional jobs they thought offered security were not truly safe. Thus, they decided to look for work that is more aligned with their genuine wants. Workers are questioning whether "safe" jobs that compromise their happiness are worth the sacrifice. Moreover, with enhanced government assistance available, it was actually *more* secure in some instances to leave an unhappy job than to stay. In a rare moment of universal clarity, many of us realized that to move forward, we had to let go.

One of the biggest difficulties in letting go of our conscious goals is that we have no guarantee better things will come our way. What if you leave your secure job, comfortable relationship, familiar city, or decent social circle and take the plunge into the unknown only to come up empty handed? For a species that hates uncertainty, this can feel like a very scary proposition, especially when we cannot predict how our desires will ever be fulfilled. Letting go requires trust.

Early in his career, Jim Carrey studied under renowned acting teacher Ivana Chubbuck. At the time, he had appeared in one television series and three movies, all of which flopped. He was on his way to being blacklisted by Hollywood.[4] Carrey was told he "overacted," so his resolution was to play his scenes small and safe. The problem, Chubbuck told him, had nothing to do with being too big or too small, it was that his onscreen persona did not reflect his true self.

A good actor is one who brings authenticity to every role. When Carrey took Ivana's advice and played his next role based on his honest desperation to be a good father, he was suddenly fun to watch. People related to him. To reach this place, however, he first had to release the personas he thought he was supposed to adopt on camera and leave himself in his rawest form. The result was the genuine, quirky Jim Carrey we all know and love today.

Time will tell whether the workers who left their jobs during the pandemic will garner similarly satisfying results. Though, with nearly 78% of job-switchers saying they're happier in their new roles, signs are looking good.[5] The question is whether you are willing to be a part of this revolution. Will you reevaluate the parts of your life that are making you unhappy? Can you let them go? Are you brave enough to try something new and trust it will work out?

The third step toward living as our true selves and attracting Mercury Mind connections is to embrace and act on our authentic attractions. This process is like the journey up to the top of a mountain.

At the base of the mountain, we can only look up through the pines, cracks, and brush to see the long trek ahead of us. We tighten the straps on our packs, lace up our shoes, and commit to the journey, trusting the view will be worth the discomfort. We may have read the guidebook, planned a route, and talked to other hikers coming down the mountain to assess the best path forward, but until we actually start climbing we cannot be truly prepared for what our personal journey will look like. As much as we believe we know what's coming, we should be prepared to let go of our beliefs about what the climb will or should be.

As we begin to trek, perhaps we'll find a fallen tree blocking our path. A certain shortcut might be frozen over during the winter or impossibly muddy during the summer. A stream that was a mere trickle in the fall may be a roaring river in the Spring. If we try to stick with our conscious plan, and persevere through these obstacles without considering other options, we might find ourselves in a treacherous situation. Letting go of a plan that no longer serves us allows us the freedom to choose the best path forward.

As we continue up the mountain, choosing our steps carefully, we may begin to realize our own limitations. The sweat may drip down our faces, our boots may rub calluses into our heels, and we may be hit upside the head with the realization we are in a suboptimal state for a hike after a holiday binge diet of beer and pepperoni pizza. When we recognize our physical condition is not where it needs to be we can either power up the mountain Rambo-style with a stitch in our side and a cramp in our calf, or accept our limitations and recalibrate our plan. If we opt for the Rambo approach, pushing through our pain to keep up with our friends, we may soon feel exhausted. We might lose our footing and stray from the path as we struggle to find the way forward. On the other hand, if we are comfortable with our physical condition, and not trying to prove anything to anyone, perhaps we will realize that we could benefit from taking a rest, scarfing down a granola bar, or shooting the breeze with another hiker for a few minutes. When we own our limitations we are better able to give ourselves what we honestly need in the moment, even as life throws unexpected challenges into our path.

Taking a break from the slog and letting our friends go on ahead, we might discover we don't really want to go to the top of the mountain anymore. Maybe we stumble upon a beautiful valley or meet a new friend who we connect with more authentically than our rah-rah Rambo buddies. Our wants constantly evolve, but as long as we keep choosing the option that aligns with our true desires, we will progressively inch closer to the real us. That destination, wherever it may be, is worth the scrapes, blood, and bruises along the way.

The Bottom of the Mountain: Releasing the Constraints

Throughout our lives, we often decide to take the safer path rather than the more authentic one. We opt for the job, relationship, and home that is more certain to win us approval, comfort, and stability, rather than truly going for what we deeply want. However, these choices often only give us the illusion of security. The miserable paper-pushing position we thought would support us financially could falter when our boss is convicted of insider trading. The boring but stable woman we thought would stay with us forever could dump us when the hunky woodcutter moves in next door. The small, shabby home we thought would keep a roof over our heads could burn down when our 1980's toaster sparks an electrical fire. Nothing in life is certain, despite our best efforts to control the future.

The reason we consistently take the safe path in life is because we believe the world around us is a fierce place. Even Jim Carrey compared the world to a wild cat biding its time until it swats us in the face. We are convinced that things could go south at any minute. If we take the exciting-looking trail that isn't marked on the map, we might be preyed on by a pack of hungry pumas. Or we could wander off the edge of a cliff. It's better to stick to the plan. We should follow the well-worn trails that are regularly maintained.

Yet, it is necessary to wander away from the safe path at times when it no longer works for us. We could find our way blocked by a massive mudslide, or overrun with daycare groups and child pick-up times, or maybe we catch a glimpse of a captivating 40-something woman in booty shorts while taking a different route. In these cases, following the new path can be more authentic than staying on the tried-and-true trail. Clinging to our initial plan often leads to frustration, disappointment, or even danger when our desires take a different path.

In his book, "Into Thin Air", journalist Jon Krauker recounts his perilous 1996 expedition up Mount Everest. His guide pushed the group onward despite several setbacks with altitude sickness, falls, and fighting between members. This persistence led to the deaths of half the party, including the guide himself.

The traumatic experience could have been avoided if the guide let go of his need to get everyone to the top. He allowed his unrelenting commitment to his conscious goal of improving his reputation as a guide take precedence over a more authentic desire to find shelter from the rapidly-approaching storm, and faced tragic consequences. He could have turned the group around when they started running low on oxygen, or when hypomania set in, or when they noticed the massive storm encroaching on the horizon. For the survivors, the guide's valuation of getting to the top over his charges' welfare was nothing short of extraordinary oversight.

We may not all be mountaineering up Everest, but we all have found ourselves in situations where it would have benefitted us to let go rather than hold on. The man in the miserable twenty year marriage may have been happier if he broke off the engagement before he ever walked down the aisle. The woman who stayed at her excruciating job as a bookkeeper could have avoided co-conspirator charges if she had quit when she realized her slimy boss was skimming off the top for his bungalow in Waikiki. Even the rodeo clown who insisted he could tame the bull could have avoided a broken leg if only he'd let go of the reins a minute earlier.

Releasing ourselves from our plan often feels unsafe, but clinging to our conscious goals can be just as dangerous. Whether we are choosing a new car, selecting a college major, or swiping through dating profiles, it's easy to convince ourselves not to go with the options that truly excite us the most. We opt for our idea of reality over intensity. But the truth is that following our authentic attractions is more likely to lead to lasting fulfillment.

We may believe there is perhaps a middle ground, and we can let go part of the way while keeping a safety line tethered around our waist. Perhaps then we could have both the promise of the attractive path and the security of the safe path. However, instead of offering us the best of both worlds, positioning ourselves between what we really want and what we think keeps us safe gives us the benefit of neither. The man who stays in an unhappy marriage yet strays off into an affair with his twenty-eight-year-old aromatherapist might think he's discovered a way to balance both safety and passion in his life. But two years later, he's sitting alone in a one-bedroom apartment with an alimony payment and an STD. The bookkeeper who keeps her shady job yet pursues her love of filming TikTok makeup tutorials on the side may believe she enjoys both job security and a creative outlet. However, when the feds come knocking, they could use her public videos featuring expensive Chanel products to bolster their claim that she, too, reaped financial benefits from her boss's money laundering scheme. The rodeo clown who keeps one hand on the horn and one foot off the saddle may think he's in a prime position to make record time and be ready to jump off. Later that night, however, he's laid up in the hospital with a broken leg and a massive groin injury.

The key to making the process of letting go work for us is to free ourselves completely from the safe path that isn't working for us. If we don't step off the path that isn't working for us, then we will never find the path that does work for us. Tying ourselves to a safe pathway that only brings us part of the way up the mountain blocks us from walking the trail that will lead us exactly where we want to go. Straying from the path that isn't serving our true desires, regardless of the outcome, gives us the opportunity to find the route that will create authentic fulfillment.

The Middle of the Mountain: Accepting Who We Are and What We Want

After letting go of the goals we've adopted to please others, we can then begin the process of surrendering to what we truly want. As we do this, it helps to pay particular attention to the desires we shy away from. These are the authentic attractions that cause us the most pain and, likely, they are most in need of our attention. We can discover these through a process of rigid self-reflection.

In the middle of our trek up the mountain, as the storm rolls in, we get low on water, and our feet begin to ache and blister, we finally reach a point where we give in to what we honestly want. We stop forcing ourselves to put one foot in front of the other and we pause to reflect on whether we really want to keep pushing forward at all. By accepting our true desire to take a break, change trails, or turn back, we can connect with our authentic self.

However, if we aren't ready to admit that we don't want to push forward, we might resort to judging and suppressing our honest desires, which leads to feelings of shame. This causes a psychological phenomenon known as reaction formation, where we seek to avoid painful emotions by gravitating toward the opposite of what we truly want. We make fun of the other hikers in our group who talk about taking a break or turning back. We challenge a friend to a race to the summit, and bet him $100 we'll get there first. Since we can't admit what we truly want, we actually force ourselves into the opposite point of view.

Reaction formation isn't just a mountain climbing phenomenon. It shows up in all walks of life. For example, a man stuck in an unhappy arranged marriage might act possessive and clingy with his wife to make himself believe he doesn't want to lose her. A jock who is attracted to a friendship with the unpopular kid in class may tease the other boy relentlessly to prove there is no connection between the two of them. The mother who feels ashamed for conceiving a child out of wedlock could become a helicopter parent to convince herself, her friends, and her therapist that she really *does* want the baby.

Typically, the desires that cause the strongest emotions in us are the ones we try the hardest to suppress. If we go so far as to *despise* someone or something, it is generally an indication that we resonate or identify with some aspect of them or it. Often, the things that cause us the most angst are reflections of our truest inner selves.

Anger, hate, and prejudice are often superficial emotions that can act as indicators for our insecurities. We project our fears onto other people because it helps us to avoid having to admit to ourselves and the people around us what we truly want. Projection is a well-studied defense mechanism in which we use other people as scapegoats to avoid expressing our own deepest feelings.[6] You can see projection most obviously in children who say things like their toy is upset with you because you put them in time out.

The woman who constantly makes fun of overweight people may herself be terrified of gaining weight because she *wants* to eat cheeseburgers for dinner and chocolate cake for breakfast. The liberal who condemns all right-wing Republicans for their inhumane border policies may fear his own sadistic impulses. The ice cream vendor who tells anyone who will listen about how Dip 'n Dots is the devil's food may secretly be insatiably drawn to the allure of the science-bending innovation.

Many people unknowingly spend their lives trapped in a shame-induced prejudice cocoon. Can you think of any similarities between you and the person you hate the most? Unfortunately, the only pathway forward is to reflect on the people, objects, and ideals we most strongly dislike. To move into our truest selves, we must admit that the very things we despise are actually reflective of our most shameful characteristics, then we can begin to accept these parts of ourselves and overcome the shame. This is ultimately how we develop impenetrable self-esteem.

It takes practice to be vulnerable about the shunned aspects of who we are. Exposing ourselves in our rawest form without lashing out at others requires serious discipline. Ultimately our impulses to lash out at people, things, and situations stems from a place of low self-esteem. It is only through acknowledging and eventually accepting the most shameful aspects of who we are that we can finally let go of our need to project these characteristics onto other people.

Often, when we acknowledge the ways in which our projections are reflective of who we truly are, we find the desires we feel so ashamed of are actually more acceptable than we believe. This is because if we have an unhealthy impulse for, say, sadistic machinations, it is indicative of a deeper desire within ourselves. In this case, it may be an impulse to concentrate on protecting our immediate family from external threats. Our desires in their deepest form are not inherently abusive, sadistic, or cruel. If they appear to be, this means we must explore deeper until we reach the true authentic attractions underneath. Acknowledging some of our less savory impulses gives us the opportunity to delve into our foundational desires. When we do this, we may find the shame we have borne for years is unfounded.

Sometimes we may not be able to dig down to the core of our attractions, no matter how hard we try. Our insatiable draw toward apple pies, computer engineering, or red-haired spectacled men may remain a mystery to us. These desires may not be reaction formation, projection, or shame. In some cases, it may take years before we can gain enough understanding of the deeper desires behind our surface level wants.

Thankfully, attempting to classify our desires into neat little boxes is unnecessary. We only have to accept these wants, admit we cannot control them, and surrender to their existence as the truest parts of ourselves. As Mary Oliver said, your only true job as a human is to "let the soft animal of your body love what it loves." When we surrender to our desires as the gifts they are, we can live more authentically, without shame.

Our attractions have a greater power over us than we have over them. And like the proverbial cork in the ice bucket, the more we push down our desires through control, avoidance, or projection, the more we build up the pressure. It will explode eventually in unhealthy ways. Our cork never stops wanting to float, so why not let it bob to the surface? Holding it down is never going to make the desire dissipate.

As humans, we gravitate toward authenticity. When we show our truths, we give ourselves the chance to be truly loved for our real selves. One common demonstration of this lies in the stories of LGBTQ+ people who have publicly embraced their true desires and found acceptance. On his 30th anniversary of coming out, Ian McKellen tweeted, "I've never met a gay person who regretted coming out – including myself. Life at last begins to make sense when you are open and honest." Indeed, his regret was not in coming out, but in that he was not able to share his truth with his parents before their passing.[7] After his confession, he garnered international fame and adoration for his iconic portrayals in film. He considered himself a better performer and human being once he revealed his true self and overcame his shame. He was an icon and will remain so for years to come.

The Top of the Mountain: Flexibly Acting On Our True Desires

As we near the top of the mountain, it is finally time to act on our true desires. When we accept our attractions in their rawest form, we can pursue them in creative ways without shame. Thankfully, we do not need to take big steps right away. We can start small with daily actions. The hiker who outlines out his entire trip and refuses to veer from his route, even when the pathway he planned to take is now flooded, will be in trouble. To avoid the over-planning folly, we can start small by making daily decisions that align with our true desires.

For example, when a woman who didn't want to be a mother is offered a position as President for her local Parent-Teacher Association, she can turn the offer down. Instead of filling her time with more activities to serve her child, she could instead accept an offer to schedule a weekly wine and cheese night with her girlfriends, giving her the reprieve from motherhood she so craves.

Small decisions can lead to big changes, but only if we are consistent in acting from our true desires. If we compromise our decisions, only partially acting from our authentic attractions, or if we fall into the trap of prioritizing our conscious wants over our true desires, we will remain unfulfilled. This is where faith once again intersects with our journey up the mountain. A mere hope things will turn around, without the daily actions to materialize desire into change, is not enough. We must act with unassailable faith, trusting our small decisions will lead us toward our true goals.

When we continuously act every day from a place of connection with our true desires, we will find our cycles naturally lead us to resolution. Though sometimes this resolution takes longer or leads us somewhere different than we could have anticipated. Perhaps our journey's destination is not to the top of the mountain after all. We might find halfway through the trek that our desire to make it to the top morphs. Maybe we planned the hike because we wanted to connect with the nature around us. Perhaps our true desire was to make a romantic connection with a fellow climber. Or we might be attracted to the idea of writing a story about the beauty of making it only halfway to our destination before turning around and going home to enjoy the view from our front porch. By allowing this flexibility in our desires, we permit ourselves the grace of an open, unpredictable, and winding road to a kind of happiness we could neither conceive nor plan for.

Indeed, substantial research shows our genuine desires naturally change throughout our lives.[8] When people are in their youth, most seek knowledge, expansion into new places, and socialization with new people. As we age, however, we seek emotional fulfillment in our work and relationships. Thus, basing our decisions off the wants of our younger selves is a futile endeavor. We must check in with our desires frequently. This is why, instead of sticking adamantly to a set of five, ten, or twenty year goals, we can simply ask ourselves whether each decision we make serves what we genuinely want *right now* or takes us further away from our true goals.

Jim Carrey could not have predicted the trajectory of his career from comic genius leading man to Golden Globe-winning dramatic movie star to pop art painter to influential philosopher; he simply kept making choices every day that aligned with his true desires. He maintained the *faith* that things would work out for him in the end. Each new version of Jim Carrey was true to his authentic attractions, and that resonated with the public, even though each incarnation may have appeared different to outsiders. As Carrey's desires changed, so too did their manifestation. The only consistency is that each version of Jim Carrey has been real.

Making decisions that appeal to our true desires, whatever they may be and however they may change, will ultimately build our self-esteem. As we keep reinforcing our true selves with decisions that appeal to our genuine wants, we will develop an intimate and loving relationship with ourselves. When we show up for our true self, it will show up for us too. This accountability will lead us to discover the greatest version of who we are.

If you're having trouble following this step on your own, you can utilize the following exercises to help you embrace your authentic wants, free from judgment, and take steps toward marked action.

Exercise #1: Letting Go

Take a deep breath; inhale for three seconds and then exhale for six. Continue to breathe in and out slowly as you relax each part of your body, one muscle at a time. First, tighten the muscle, then let it go. Start with your forehead, moving down to your eyebrows, nose, mouth, then jawbone. Scrunch the muscle as hard as you can while you draw in a lungful of air, then release the breath, letting the tension melt away under your skin until the muscle feels soft and heavy.

Once you're fully relaxed, ask yourself the following questions. You may notice emotions like shame, guilt, or anger arise. Accept these emotions and then go into them further to understand what might be causing them. Your answers are simply your truth, they are neither good nor bad.

To disentangle yourself from these emotions, imagine the person answering these questions is not actually you, but a different version of yourself who is already living in their truth. We'll call them Person A. You know nothing about Person A's job, current relationships, home, or friends. All you know is their answers are true. After this encounter, you have no obligation to them and they have none to you.

Now, ask Person A:

What are you pursuing in your life to impress other people? What romantic relationships, career aspirations, friendships, possessions, and forms of social status are you aspiring to because you believe they will make other people like you more?

Spend five minutes listing out as many answers as you possibly can. When five minutes are up, consider all of your responses carefully and choose one that feels most important. You might select the thing you spend the most time thinking about, or invest the most money toward, or feel the worst about not having. Don't over analyze this. Just relax and use your gut to select the thing that feels most important.

How do you feel when you think about letting go of this aspiration? Is it a relief on some level?

As you imagine Person A answering these questions, remove your judgment on their responses. There is nothing wrong with any type of aspirations. We all pursue things that we think will make us more attractive to others. Allow Person A space to fully explore what it would feel like to let go of these desires.

You may feel immediate resistance to the thought of releasing

such an important pursuit. All of those muscles you worked to systematically relax at the start of the exercise might tense back up again
now. After all, you've likely spent many hours dreaming up how to get
this thing (and feeling bad for not already having it). In these cases, the
pursuit becomes a large part of our identity. If we stop going after this
goal, who will we be?

Spend another five minutes fully imagining what it would feel like
to let go of this goal. Likely, it would be strange. But would you also
feel a sense of peace? Would your life be a bit more authentic?

Once you feel you've let go, or begun to let go of your false
desires, you can move on to the second exercise.

Exercise #2: Acknowledging Our Deepest Desires

For the next exercise, begin again by tensing and relaxing your
entire body. Breathe in and out as you progressively clench and then
release each muscle, starting from the top of your head and working
your way down to your toes.

Take a few moments to reflect on the people and events over the
last week that caused you the most grief. What has caused you stress?
What have you worried about most? What are you unable to stop
turning over in your mind?

Imagine Person A is someone who acts on the things you obsess
over. For example, if you are pissed off about the inequity in your
romantic relationship, but don't want to make a big deal over it,
imagine Person A calls your partner out on her behavior and ends the
partnership. If you obsess over the hot neighbor next door, imagine
Person A has a torrid love affair with him. If you can't stop worrying
about the daily stresses of your workplace, imagine Person A quit
three years ago and is now happily employed, doing your dream job.
Ask yourself the following questions.

*If Person A had traded places with you for the past year, what would be
different about your life today? What are the changes Person A would have made
that you have been resisting?*

If you decided to live more like Person A, starting today, would
you feel more authentic or less authentic? What did you discover
about your true desires by imagining Person A taking over your life for
a while? Find somewhere to be alone for a moment. Take a deep

breath and repeat: "It is ok to want this." No justifications. No apologies. No conditions. Only a simple acceptance.

This is not to say that you need to take action on your wants right away. The helicopter parent with the unwanted child does not have to give the kid up to the local firehouse. The clingy man with the wife he isn't into doesn't need to ask for a divorce right away. The high school jock doesn't need to ask the kid he's been bullying to hang out and play video games. Simply admitting these attractions to yourself and accepting them is a huge step. It's ok to want these things. You have nothing to be ashamed of.

Remember, our Mercury Mind attractions are a wholly natural part of who we are as humans. We cannot control them and because of this, they represent the most organic parts of us. You were made exactly as you are and the only pathway forward is to see and accept this.

Once you have been able to uncover at least one authentic desire, free from judgment, the exciting part begins: taking action toward living more genuinely.

Exercise #3: Taking Action

Think of one genuine desire you recognized while reading this chapter. Make a vow to yourself that, from now on, any time you face a relevant decision, you will act from this genuine desire. Even if it is as simple as choosing whether or not to grab a cup of coffee, ask yourself: Does this action feed my true attractions, or does it detract from them?

From now on, commit to acting from your honest desires in everything you do. Remind yourself frequently to stay true to your authentic attractions. At the end of each day, record the changes you see in your life. After a month, take twenty minutes to journal about all of the changes you've seen in your life when acting from this place of your genuine desires.

This should become a continual process of reflection and action. It is a daily meditation that will lead you ever-closer to your true self.

Take a hard look at where you are right now. It may not feel good. But you can trust in the coming weeks and months of this practice, the view will broaden as you open up possibilities through a fuller expression of yourself. The blues, reds, and purples of the sky above you will deepen as you climb further up the mountain, and you will see more of the expanse of valleys, rivers, and forests below. When you reach your apex, wherever that may be, you will finally know more of yourself than ever before.

9

Healthy Actions Inspire
Healthy Relationships

It's great to release ourselves from our inauthentic wants and connect with our true attractions, but as we set out to actually pursue our desires we encounter another issue. What if the things we most honestly crave are unhealthy for ourselves or for other people? What if we are attracted to relationships that will sabotage our goals, go against our values, or harm our loved ones? We can't merely set out to pursue whatever strikes our fancy in life without pausing for a moment to consider whether the actions we are about to take are healthy for everyone involved.

Some friends of mine illustrate the problems that can arise from allowing our passions to drive us unchecked. Let's call them Janet and Dave. After three relatively happy years of marriage, this hip young New York City couple was on the brink of a divorce. Before the COVID-19 pandemic, their only issues had been minor disagreements about things like dirty dishes, football teams, and where to get dinner. When New York issued a mandatory citywide quarantine, Janet and Dave anticipated few, if any, problems. They blissfully hunkered down in their ninth floor studio loft with dirty gin martinis and *Tiger King* cued up on Netflix. However, they were about to experience the incredible power of self-sabotage first hand.

After three months of isolation, Janet felt the immense weight of disconnection from the outside world. As the more extroverted member of the pair, she grew increasingly irritable the longer she remained cut off from friends and family. Dave, to avoid his wife's outbursts, withdrew.

Feeling abandoned, Janet took to daydreaming about connections outside of their marriage. One day, she came across the Facebook page of her college boyfriend, Jared. She commented on his photo and, five minutes later he sent her a like. Soon, they were messaging every day. Then they *just happened* to run into each other at the supermarket and got to talking. This led to a steamy affair.

As Janet grew closer with Jared, Dave made more plans without her, talked to her less, and took long road trips by himself. While Janet had initially felt Jared's connection gave her what was missing from her marriage, she soon remembered why she'd ended things with Jared a decade prior. Their old relationship issues began to resurface —his lying, their blowout fights, and her crushing insecurity. Soon, Janet felt even more isolated than before.

By pursuing intimacy outside her marriage, Janet actually undermined her genuine desire for a deeper connection. While there's nothing wrong with yearning for closeness, Janet used self-sabotaging tactics to get what she wanted. It was not her desire for connection, but the actions she took to pursue it, that were unhealthy.

Janet's story illustrates that pursuing our authentic desires is a complicated undertaking. Sometimes, we get what we want at the expense of our values, relationships, and overall well-being. In the words of renowned business philosopher Jim Rohn, "Beware of what you become in pursuit of what you want."

In pursuing our desires, we may become someone we don't want to be. Consider the teenage girl who longs to lose weight, but does it by forcing herself to vomit after every meal. She gets the toned tummy she sought, but makes herself unhealthy in the process. Or think of the dad who promises to protect his child from bullies, but does it by teaching his kid how to sucker punch, transforming the boy into a tyrant. Or envision the entrepreneur who aspires to build the best pet shop on the block, but does it by purchasing puppies from unscrupulous doggy mills. He may get the pets he needs, but at the cost of supporting unethical breeders.

Often we may be able to get what we want, but at a steep personal cost. The question is whether we are willing to pay the price. Our actions can sometimes be misguided. We can follow our attractions down a dangerous road. How, then, do we choose the right *actions* to get what we want while staying true to our values?

As we begin our journey to realizing our authentic attractions, we should recognize it is not our desires that get us into hot water, but the unhealthy actions we take in pursuing those desires. Janet's craving for connection isn't wrong, but jumping into bed with Jared wasn't a healthy choice. If we analyze this closer, we can see Janet has succumbed to the anxiety of uncertainty and forced a cycle closed, much to her detriment.

While we may not have control over our authentic attractions, we do decide which actions we take to achieve them. The onus is therefore on us to take responsibility for the self-sabotaging things we do as we chase after the things we want.

Self-sabotage is sometimes easier on our psyche in the short term than taking on the weight of responsibility. For example, when Janet recognized she felt lonely, she could have accepted that she had played a role in causing her feelings. She didn't reach out to friends, failed to communicate her feelings in an open way, and ultimately alienated her husband with her ill temper. Instead of holding herself responsible, however, she chose to engage in further self-sabotage by pursuing connection in a destructive way.

If Janet had taken responsibility, she may have opened herself up to healthier actions to meet her needs. For instance, she could have sat Dave down and explained what she needed from him. She could have said, "Dave, I'm feeling insecure in our relationship and I want to feel like part of a community again." This display of vulnerability may have opened her up to a deeper level of intimacy with Dave, thus strengthening their marriage. Then, together, they might have found ways to meet her needs, whether through more Zoom calls with friends, or a deeper level of communication between the two of them.

Accepting responsibility for our current situation is the first key to avoiding self-sabotage as we pursue our authentic attractions. In order to pursue our desires in a *healthy* way, we must admit that the actions we've taken in the past have failed to achieve our goals.

What Makes A Healthy Action

While our authentic desires are natural and healthy, the actions we take to achieve them are not always beneficial. One big reason for this is that our actions can be distorted by our longing to prematurely close our cycles. In a rush to satisfy our wants, we can make decisions that are destructive rather than constructive.

Frankie genuinely wants a safe home for his wife and kids. However, in his haste to buy a house in the right neighborhood, he takes out a loan from his parents. This leaves his family indebted to his folks for the next decade and he feels obligated to go out of his way to help them, even if it means he isn't about to spend much time with his own children. He allows his parents to move in with his family for a year while they downsize to a condo, which puts stress on Frankie's marriage. Ironically, the actions he took to keep his family secure backfired. He ended up spending less time with his wife and kids and feeling more stressed out.

Like Frankie, when we choose unhealthy actions in pursuit of our authentic desires, we engage in self-sabotage. This pattern is generally driven by low self-esteem. The less we value ourselves, the more pressure we feel to close the cycle as quickly as possible. Because Frankie does not truly believe he is the kind of man who can provide a safe home for his family, he jumps at the first opportunity he comes across to buy a house. Instead of waiting patiently for the right deal to come along, he goes for the option that affords the most instant gratification.

If Frankie had been more secure in his ability to provide his family with a safe home, he may have been comfortable slowing down, sitting in a bit of uncertainty, and waiting for a better housing opportunity. He could have spent a few years saving up enough capital to put a down payment on a loan with a better interest rate and not found himself obligated to acquiesce to every request his parents made. Although this may have taken longer, Frankie would have freed his family of stressful obligations and been able to maintain stress-free relations with both his parents and children.

Actions born out of high self-esteem are often constructive, whereas actions born out of low self-esteem are often destructive. When we are secure in who we are, it's safe to wait patiently and leave the cycle open. However, if we don't feel good about ourselves, it's tempting to accept the first opportunity to close the cycle.

One simple way to assess whether we are pursuing our attractions in a healthy way is to ask ourselves how we feel about the actions we are taking. When Frankie went to his parents asking for money he felt ashamed. Alternatively, if he would have patiently worked hard to amass sufficient funds for a good home, he could feel proud of his accomplishment.

Janet similarly felt embarrassed when she was messaging Jared, whereas she felt authentic sharing her true feelings with Dave. When she crawled into bed next to her husband after meeting up with Jared at two in the morning, she felt guilty snuggling up against the man who seemed so far apart from her now. When she finally came clean about her needs, Janet initially felt vulnerable and exposed. But by owning her feelings and exposing her raw self to Dave she opened her cycle of connection back up again. She had no idea how he would respond and this uncertainty made her anxious. However, this level of vulnerability also felt much more authentic and was aligned with her true values.

Actions and Our Value System

At times, it can be difficult to distinguish whether our actions reflect high or low self-esteem. None of us want to admit we have a low-self-worth. We're good at convincing ourselves we feel great about who we are. Because of this human tendency, reflecting on our level of self-esteem is not always a reliable way to distinguish between healthy or unhealthy actions. We need another strategy.

One simple method we can employ to measure whether our actions are constructive or destructive is weighing our behaviors against our core value system. When we notice ourselves being easily pulled away from our core values, that's an indication that we don't value ourselves enough to stand firm in our beliefs. Thus, the level of alignment between our actions and our value system is a good barometer of our self-value, or self-esteem.

Like authentic desires, our value system is not set in stone. Values can and do change throughout our lifetimes and are a reflection of what is most important to us currently. We can weigh our values against our behaviors to assess whether we are acting in line with our value system. For example, if your heart says you should never withstand a toxic relationship, yet you continue showing up at your borderline girlfriend's house every night with a black eye and a bottle of wine, then your actions are not reflective of your value system. Or if your mind says family always comes first, yet you've missed the last three of your son's baseball games for emergency work meetings, then you are out of alignment with your beliefs. Or if your gut tells you the politician you are voting for is a crook, yet you vote for this person anyway because everyone in your immediate circle is doing it, then you are going against your own morals.

If your *actions* are out of alignment with your value system, there are two potential explanations. One possibility is that your values are out of alignment with your deepest desires. For instance, you might be telling yourself that you value community when you're actually more authentically attracted to independence. In this case, the solution is to get honest with yourself about what you truly value.

The other possibility when your actions and values don't match is that your behaviors might be an unhealthy reflection of your true desires. For example, Sandra's top conscious priority might be building an app for cat owners who want to get their pets into the film industry. In her heart, Sandra wants to find ways of bringing others joy. She is trying to do this by giving pet owners an avenue to see their adorable kittens on the big screen. But how does her behavior align with her honest values?

When Sandra wins a prestigious grant, she squanders the money on an expensive developer who creates a slow, confusing app for animal casting directors that crashes after every fourth swipe. Instead of cutting her losses and finding a new developer who can build the kind of platform that will bring her patrons joy, Sandra pays the same developer to create another version. This iteration overcharges subscribers, leading to a slew of cancellations, complaints, and threats. Not wanting to admit her mistake, she takes out a credit card to give the developer *even more* money for a third version, which ends up being a nearly exact duplicate of the first with an annoying Meow Mix track added in. The few customers Sandra has left are not impressed.

Sandra really *does* want her "Cats on Cue" app to be successful, but she is sabotaging herself through her actions. When she continues to invest in this shoddy developer despite the failures, she prioritizes her pride over her value system. She has an authentic attraction to spreading joy through furry felines. After the third app prototype failure, however, she is only spreading frustration.

Sandra cannot take responsibility for her missteps, thus leading her into a perpetual cycle of self-sabotage. Avoiding responsibility may temporarily ease her discomfort. However, by choosing actions that move her farther away from her value system, she devalues herself and lowers her self-esteem. This leads her to take even more actions that stem from a place of insecurity, causing a downward spiral.

When Sandra first realized her app was yielding more exasperation for her patrons than exuberance, she could have measured this truth against her value system and found her actions weren't matching up. At that point there are many things she could have done to bring her behavior and values back into alignment. For example, she could have found a new developer, consulted with app patrons to see what would make the app most enjoyable, promised users a free month of membership for the overcharging snafu, or scrapped the app idea altogether and found a different way to spread joy to animal lovers. Instead, she ignored the discrepancy, and marched further down the path of her conscious plan.

Taking responsibility for actions that contradict our values empowers us to change our actions. Without this ownership, however, we are doomed to a perpetual cycle of self-sabotage. To take responsibility for our actions, we need to identify when they are in opposition to our value system. And this level of self-awareness is not easy to muster. Perhaps our value system isn't as clear-cut as "spread joy to as many people as possible." In those cases, we can run our actions through a litmus test of "red flags" to see whether any of our behaviors conflict with our values.

The following are some of the potential indicators that your actions and values may be out of alignment:

The action causes you shame.

If you feel guilty about your behavior, then it is likely out of alignment with your values. This is doubly true if no one else ever knows about what you've done. For example, if Josiah has an affair no one will ever find out about, but he still wakes up every night for a week afterward drenched in a cold sweat, this behavior is likely out of alignment with his values. We are often good at convincing ourselves logically that we are ok with something. But we can't talk ourselves out of emotions. When you feel shame about something you've done it's a good indication your actions aren't 100% in alignment with your beliefs about what's right and wrong.

Similarly, if we feel we have to hide our actions from people, particularly those we love, we may be feeling shame. For example, if Mark is shooting up in the bathroom every night away from the prying eyes of his girlfriend, it is likely an indication he feels shame over his actions. If he was proud of his behavior he wouldn't feel the need to hide it. Shame usually indicates a broken value system.

The action hurts other people.

If you do something that causes others to experience pain, you might be acting outside your value system. For example, if Delilah wants to grow her career as a life coach, but her strategy for attracting clients is to cut down other local life coaches on social media, then she's probably not acting authentically. While there is nothing wrong with Delilah's desire to build her business, there is clearly a problem with her marketing tactics because they are causing distress to her competitors. Unless harming others is a core value for her, Delilah needs to change this behavior if she wants to live in alignment with her inner truth.

One important caveat to this rule involves people who are just toxic. If, for example, your mother says she's heartbroken over your choice of relationship, that doesn't mean your love for your partner is wrong. You're not directly doing anything to harm your mother. In fact, she's being manipulative by blaming her pain on you. We'll cover this type of situation more in the next chapter.

The action appeals to other people's morals, not your own.

If we serve other people's value systems to the degradation of our own, we are often engaging in self-destructive behavior. In the midst of the COVID-19 pandemic, many people faced this dilemma as loved ones chose where they stood on masks, quarantines, and vaccines. This led some to alter their personal convictions in an effort to align themselves with their friends. In fact, a recent survey found the most important predictor of vaccine status was peer-pressure.[1] People mostly went along with what their friends were doing. As a result, many people put themselves in painful, uncomfortable, and even downright dangerous situations to avoid rocking the boat with loved ones instead of acting in a way that aligned with their own value systems.

The action satisfies one true desire, but roadblocks another.

Not all actions are created equal, and sometimes we choose behaviors that serve one authentic desire but defile another. We may not be able to conceive of actions that can serve two desires authentically, so we give up and sacrifice one of our attractions in an effort to close the cycle. However, if we have patience, a solution will often present itself that is in line with all of our values.

Eunice was struggling with this type of value conflict. She didn't attend her good friend Alan's birthday bowling bash because his boyfriend made an inappropriate comment about her beach photo on Instagram a few days before. Although Eunice values being a good friend, she also values being respected by the people in her life. Her action of staying at home rather than attending Alan's party may have supported her value of demanding respect, but not her desire to be there for her friends. In this case, she had the opportunity to take an action that satisfied both values. She could have attended the party and kept her distance from the boyfriend. She could have expressed her concerns privately to Alan. Or she could have even told his boyfriend honestly how his comments made her feel. Expressing herself may have helped her feel comfortable enough to support her friend.

An action that sacrifices one desire over another is not a sign of virtuousness, it represents a lack of creativity at best and cowardice at worst.

The action is addictive, not obsessive.

Mercury Mind attractions are extremely intense. When we gravitate toward our authentic desires, they will naturally flood our thoughts and shape our ambitions. It is normal for us to obsess over what we truly want in life. However, when our obsessive thoughts turn into addictive actions, they cross the line from a healthy pursuit of our wants into long-term self-sabotage.

In an obsessive state we might be wholly preoccupied with a pursuit, but this does not mean we will necessarily chase our desires at the expense of our values. We can be crazy about someone and still hold firm to our values. When a desire crosses over into an addiction, however, we'll do anything to get what we want, no matter the cost. Thus, one sign of an addiction is that it supersedes our value system.

Addictions can lead to self-sabotage when we can't see any other way to fulfill our desires. When we feel this way, it is often a reflection of low self-esteem. A famous example of this is the story of Pattie Boyd. In the late 1960's, The Beatles rockstar George Harrison started working with Eric Clapton, who soon became obsessed with George's wife, Pattie, eventually penning his famous song "Layla" in tribute to her. When she rebuffed his advances, however, Clapton sunk into a deep depression, self-imposed isolation, and a nasty heroin addiction.[2] Eric turned to drugs because he believed there was no other way to assuage his need for Pattie's love. As a result, he hurt himself, his musical career, and his friendships, compromising his ethical integrity.

Ironically, upon sobering up he lived with, and eventually married, Pattie Boyd. The Mercury Mind Attraction turned into a Mercury Mind Connection when Clapton accepted his authentic self and chose healthy actions to boost his self-esteem.

By running our behaviors through this value system "red flags" checklist, we can identify which actions will serve us, and which may lead us ever-further away from what we truly want.

Of course, it is rarely just one individual action, but a pattern of behavior that determines whether a *relationship* becomes healthy or toxic.

Self-Sabotage in Action

Self-sabotage can show up in different ways in all three types of relationships. Thankfully, there are some simple healthy alternatives we can implement when we notice ourselves committing any form of self-sabotage. The difficult part is getting honest with ourselves about where our behaviors are potentially unhealthy or misaligned with our values.

Business Relationships

Our professional relationships often turn toxic when we make wayward choices to appeal to our coworkers, ambitions, or bosses. When we consistently serve others to get what we want, we can lose sight of the values at our foundation. This might come in the form of sacrificing sleep to finish up a big project. Or maybe we find ourselves bending our morals to close a big deal. Or we could notice we are kissing up to our asshole boss because we think it will land us a promotion.

Consider Charles, who is an environmental engineer, excited about the invitation from his manager to hang out after work. Dominic, his manager, insists they meet at a strip bar, which seems a little shady to Charles, but, shrugging his shoulders, Charles agrees and hopes for the best.

After a few hours at the strip club, Charles finds it's not so uncomfortable when he focuses on he and Dominic's conversation rather than the dancing girls. But then, in the middle of a group strip number, Dominic drags Charles into the bathroom and whips out a little bag of white powder. Charles's eyes bug out as Dominic suggests they do a few lines of coke. Wanting his manager's approval, Charles feels he has no choice but to partake. But in the morning, Charles feels rotten, not just because of the hangover, but because of his choices.

The decision to acquiesce to his manager's domineering requests creates a toxic relationship for Charles. He could have taken healthy action by changing the direction of the evening. He could have authentically expressed his discomfort about going to a strip club, and suggested they meet at a sports pub instead. He could have reinforced a professional relationship by keeping the conversation focused on how he appreciated the manager's mentorship. He could have faked a cold instead of going out in the first place!

As soon as Charles allowed himself to behave in ways that went against his values, he engaged in self-sabotage.

Platonic Relationships

With our friends and family members there are two main ways relationships can devolve into self-sabotage. Either we can prioritize certain people too far above our other desires or, alternatively, we can take people for granted and prioritize our other desires above them. Both of these situations are unhealthy and can lead to self-sabotage.

Jenny is a proud mother who says her son is her whole world. However, when Jenny meets a group of moms at her son's new elementary school, she signs up for a weekly "mom's night out." A few weeks later, Johnny reminds mom that they had plans to see the premiere of the newest superhero movie. But Jenny digs her heels in and thinks, *I deserve this night off!* She leaves little Johnny at home with a babysitter. As Jenny flakes on more plans with Johnny, he stops asking her to do anything and stops reaching out to her for support. Eventually, Johnny resents his mom for her absence, turning from a boy with good sense to one who disobeys the rules in order to get attention.

In this case, Jenny faced a conflict between two desires: being a loving parent and cultivating meaningful friendships. These relationships both became toxic because she treated them as a trade-off. She viewed the two choices as dichotomous: either she could have friends, or she could be a good mom, and so she failed to see how this duplicity created toxicity. Her continual actions to dismiss her friends during the first years of Johnny's life, and then her actions to dismiss Johnny now, created unbalanced relationships. She could have, alternatively, pursued healthy relationships by creating time and space for both her friends and her son. Her choice of action was her responsibility.

Romantic Relationships

If we want a deep and lasting romantic relationship to work, we need to be ok with a high degree of vulnerability. We can't create intimacy if we never share our authentic attractions with another person. If we put up barriers between ourselves and our lovers, we will sabotage our romantic relationships.

Sammy was a carpenter whose work allowed him to provide a nice home for his wife, Anais. One day, Sammy injured himself on the job. Afraid he would no longer be able to give Anais a comfortable life, he downplayed his injury. Even though Sammy progressively developed more pain in his leg, he continued to hide his hurt, refusing to show a noticeable limp at home. As a result of his chronic pain, every dollar he spent took on greater importance. Soon he resented his wife for her 'outrageous' needs every time she wanted him to take her out to a nice dinner, buy her a gift, or whisk her away for a weekend vacation.

Since Sammy never communicated about his injury to Anais, she did not understand why he became progressively more irritable. He sabotaged his relationship by avoiding telling his wife what he was feeling. Rather than getting vulnerable, Sammy prioritized his desire to support her financially. As a hands-on physical worker, he was embarrassed to admit he was in pain. However, if Sammy would have shared what he was going through Anais would have had the opportunity to empathize and then help brainstorm other solutions. They would have felt more connected rather than slowly drifting apart. Healthy actions in romantic relationships are rooted in vulnerability.

Create Healthy Relationships Out of Toxic Situations

It might seem intimidating to repair toxic relationships, but it's not impossible. We have the power to find healthier ways of connecting with the people and things in our lives. Even if we are caught in a toxic pattern of communication, we can pull ourselves out. It starts by realizing that we've been sabotaging ourselves, and then taking responsibility for doing something differently.

If we are facing self-sabotaging relationships, there are four things we can do to change our actions and create healthier connections.

1. Our desire isn't the problem.

We can never be vulnerable with others if we don't fully accept our own authentic attractions. When we find ourselves sabotaging a relationship, the desire behind our actions isn't the problem. We have no more power to control our authentic wants than a tiger has to change the pattern of his stripes. So we shouldn't shame ourselves for what we want. Through humility, we can build the emotional strength to accept the desire behind the toxic relationship. When we accept this desire and stop shaming ourselves for feeling a certain way, we open up new possible ways of satisfying our needs.

2. Taking responsibility for our actions.

While we cannot control our desires, we can control our *actions*. In acknowledging this, we take responsibility for creating the self-sabotaging relationship in the first place. This may cause us to feel shame about our less-than-savory past behavior, but the idea isn't to launch into a guilt trip. The most important result of taking ownership for our actions is to realize we have the power to change our future.

Failure to take responsibility, as in the case of Janet, leads to excuses and deflection, which ultimately lowers our self-esteem. On the other hand, taking ownership leads to valuing ourselves more deeply. From a place of enhanced self-esteem we have a greater sense of power over our actions and can accept full responsibility for the relationships we develop.

Even if we are in a relationship with a toxic person, we don't have to view ourselves as victims. This view is disempowering. Victims don't have a strong sense of self-worth. Instead, we can honestly recognize that, while this person may be toxic, our actions still played a part in creating the relationship. Our craving for connection isn't wrong but the toxic patterns we have engaged in to satisfy that desire are at least partially our own responsibility.

3. Pacing ourselves against the power of attraction.

While we don't need to quell, crush, or wrangle our desires into submission, we can govern how we go about attaining our wants through discipline. Self-control when it comes to our actions allows us to behave with conscious intent toward our attractions instead of *reacting* on impulse. Reacting is what gets us in hot water as we are pulled to disregard our value systems and rush to close our cycles and get what we want as quickly as possible.

For many of us caught in a Mercury Mind obsessive state, it may be a tall order to request patient action. However, we can circumvent our reactive nature by exposing ourselves incrementally to our attractions until we can successfully control our reactions.

Take, for example, the methods employed in exposure therapy. In this type of therapy, a phobic patient is exposed incrementally to their greatest fear until they are able to control their reaction of terror. An arachnophobic patient may be initially shown a picture of a spider one day, then the next week exposed to a spider in a closed container, until one day they can tolerate a tarantula crawling up their arm. Research shows this therapy is immensely effective at reducing reactive fear responses.[3]

We can employ a similar approach to our attractions. After all, obsessive attraction and phobia are both rooted in reactions we can't control. Therapists have applied this therapy to addictions, using Pavlovian conditioning to associate a negative feeling with the addictive substance. However, since obsessions are natural manifestations of our true desires, we do not want to create negative associations with them. In fact, this can lead to feelings of shame around our true desires.

Alternatively, we can give ourselves the space to find healthy ways of acting on our obsessive desires through incremental exposure. For example, if Rowan is attracted to the cute checkout girl at the local grocery store, but he is in a monogamous marriage, he has a conflict. Acting on his attraction would damage his marriage. Instead of making daily visits to the grocery store, he could start by going to a different grocery store, only making occasional trips to see the cute checkout girl every other week. After these exposures, he could bring this sexual energy home to his wife. Eventually, he can incrementally make more trips to the grocery store as his attraction becomes less aligned with the check out girl and more aligned with his wife.

4. Develop discipline so any action is a choice.

Discipline means any action is a choice for which we take 100% responsibility. When any action becomes a choice, we can consciously decide whether our actions help us toward our desires or not. We can assess whether a specific action honestly aligns with our value system and opt for behaviors that support the growth of our self-esteem, instead of its destruction. We can even choose not to act on a desire, recognizing a perhaps deeper desire to resist and redirect this want so we can explore it in a healthy way.

Discipline is a continual process of training and tweaking. Growth comes through patience, practice, and an openness to the rawest manifestation of ourselves.

Despite everything we can do to create healthy relationships in our lives, free of self-sabotage, the truth is that relationships are not one-sided. While our own actions can be nourishing manifestations of our true desires, other people's actions may be toxic. Managing these toxic relationships when they are outside our control is a whole other skillset.

The Other Person In the Relationship

Sometimes even though we accept our authentic wants, share them with vulnerability, and act with integrity, a relationship can still fail. No matter how true we are to ourselves, or how open we are with our partner, or how much we respect them, we still have to account for the other person in the relationship. Even if we take all the right steps, it does not guarantee the other person will do the same.

Consider the true story of Marty Markowitz and his therapist, Dr. Isaac "Ike" Herschkopf. In 2010, Marty Markowitz laid in his bed, waiting for a phone call that never came. In excruciating pain after his hernia operation, Marty expected the most important person in his life, Dr. Ike, to "give a rat's ass" that he had undergone surgery. He would later describe the realization that this man he loved so much had abandoned him as a feeling "like sticking a knife into my stomach and twisting it." In those lonely days following his procedure, Marty realized what many in abusive relationships come to discover—he was not the problem.

Over the previous twenty-seven years, Dr. Ike was Marty's primary, and often sole, confidant. In the beginning of their relationship, Marty took the right action. When he first sought out professional help, on the advice of his rabbi, his parents had recently died, leaving him to manage the lucrative family fabric business amidst a swell of familial in-fighting. Marty honestly wanted a trustworthy confidant who would be on his side to help him build the self-respect and esteem necessary to run the company with confidence. He found that person in Dr. Ike. The therapist encouraged Marty to express his emotions, confide his true wants, and pursue the respect he so desperately wanted. It seemed Marty had found the friend he truly wanted.

Unfortunately, Dr. Ike had different intentions for their relationship. While Marty perceived Dr. Ike's interest in him as a genuine attraction that satisfied his true wants, Dr. Ike's objective was to manipulate, belittle, and dominate Marty into financial gain. Over time, Dr. Ike perverted the friendship through unscrupulously testing the bounds of the doctor-patient relationship, encouraging Marty to sever ties with family, instilling himself as the head of Marty's family company, and hosting lavish parties at Marty's Southampton estate. The relationship that initially helped Marty feel cared for, seen, and protected soon left him drained, embittered, and oppressed. And at the end, despite Marty's enduring trust, affection, and generosity, Dr. Ike couldn't be bothered to simply pick up the phone when his 'friend' was in need. It didn't matter how much Marty cared for Dr. Ike, the man would never love him back. It simply wasn't in his nature.

While we can do the hard work of figuring out what we want and taking the healthy actions to pursue relationships that meet those desires, we may forget there are at least two people present in any Mercury Mind connection. Although we are responsible for our own decisions, making good choices cannot coerce the other people in the relationship to do the same. We cannot force someone to show us respect. We cannot compel everyone in our lives to be truthful, kind, or open with us. We cannot love someone into loving us.

The abusive parent won't flip the switch to suddenly become the kind caretaker her children need her to be. The borderline girlfriend will not magically transform into a stable source of affection. The megalomaniac manager will not stop berating his employees and become a supportive boss overnight.

That's the mistake Marty, and so many of us, make. We forget how a person feels and acts toward us is not something we can ultimately control. Their behavior is up to them. And often, when toxicity is ingrained in other people's nature, they choose not to change. When that happens we only have two healthy choices: adjust our expectations for the relationship, or walk away.

To make this decision from a more informed place, we have to learn how to truly see the other person in the relationship for what they are, in spite of an overpowering Mercury Mind connection. We have to see past our subconscious emotional attraction and assess the true nature of the other individual. And that's not easy.

Taking the Blinders Off

We do not form relationships in a vacuum. While on our journey to attracting more Mercury Mind connections, we can do everything authentically and respectfully and still fail to build the type of relationship we seek. We can do the hard work to express our authentic desires to the other person. We can choose actions that honor our value systems. We can systematically undress layer by layer until we reveal our true selves in all our raw, imperfect glory. However, our vulnerability is not a mutual contract. There is no guarantee the other person will likewise give us the same gift of expressing their authentic selves. We cannot make them abandon their attraction to deception, distrust, or disguise. It is up to us, therefore, not to direct the person, but to decide whether this person is helping us build a constructive or destructive partnership.

Often, we are blinded by our Mercury Mind attractions. Our insatiable obsession for another person can shield us from seeing who they really are. To have a healthy, loving relationship, it serves us to be aware not only of how a person does meet our authentic desires, but how they might inhibit us from fulfilling our wants.

In the case of Marty and Dr. Ike, Marty saw only how Dr. Ike could be the connection he needed to weather a difficult, lonesome period in his life. He did not see the other aspects of Dr. Ike that detracted from his true desires. While Dr. Ike promised to help protect Marty from friends, girlfriends, and family members who only valued his fortune, he also amassed $6 million from Marty over their years working together. Dr Ike convinced Marty to rewrite his will to leave assets to the Herschkopf family and jostled Marty into making him a cosigner on a Swiss bank account. While Dr. Ike swore to help Marty garner respect, he made Marty essentially act as a manservant for his guests at extravagant get-togethers and parties. While Dr. Ike promised to help Marty shoulder the avalanche of responsibility in taking over the family business after his parent's death, in reality he made business decisions on Marty's behalf, making him less able to bear responsibility himself.

Dr. Ike's duplicitous nature magnified and multiplied over time. However, Marty's Mercury Mind attraction to Dr. Ike led him to over-commit to their relationship. Thus, when these red flags did appear, Marty dug his heels in to improve the relationship instead of questioning whether Dr. Ike's connection with him was still beneficial.

Often, our devotion to the Mercury Mind connection can supersede our commitment to ourselves. If we prioritize the relationship with another person above our relationship with ourselves, we will lose sight of what we truly want. In the case of Marty, he became so infatuated with what he thought the relationship with Dr. Ike gave him that he lost sight of how the partnership drained him, both financially and emotionally. While Marty initially felt a surge of support, with time he lost his family, friends, and reputation.

When we prioritize the desires of another person, we devalue ourselves. We signal to that person they are so important to us we will sacrifice all other potential wants to maintain our relationship with them. This might be ok if that person is as kind and generous as we are, but often, this type of blind trust attracts people who will take advantage of us.

It's why the 'nice girl' ends up with a guy who manipulates her into apologizing to him when he is the one who flaked on plans. It's why the good kid takes the fall for his friends pulling the fire alarm. It's why the employee will put in ten hours of unpaid overtime for a boss who barely acknowledges she's sacrificed her personal life for his company. In each of these scenarios, the person hurts themselves to preserve the relationship.

But is this sacrifice necessary? Is it even worth it? Often not. The sacrifice is usually largely unappreciated and creates a pattern of pain that progressively gets worse. The nice girl endures years of gaslighting, betrayal, and devaluation at the hands of her boyfriend. Eventually, she doesn't trust herself to make even the simplest decisions. The pushover friend is constantly being blamed for things he didn't do. Eventually, he racks up a criminal record and is unable to get into college. Without so much as a raise, the selfless employee works herself into the ground missing birthdays, kid's soccer games, and Christmases. She may keep her job, but she loses her personal relationships.

Some people will try to hurt us no matter how many second chances we give them.

One way to avoid this fate is to put our own wants above the needs of the relationship as long as we are not compromising vulnerability, trust, or respect in the process. By prioritizing our desires over preserving a connection, we can see a clearer, fuller picture of the relationship. If we're not spending our efforts trying to keep the other person happy, we discover who this person truly is instead of who we want them to be. We can then determine whether this relationship is genuinely helping or hurting us and assess whether it is even worth our continued investment. Or, it is also possible that our Mercury Mind attractions have shifted and the relationship is not meant to be.

When the nice girl speaks out against her boyfriend's beratements, she may find he isn't even interested in her if she's not willing to play the punching bag. When the pushover friend stops taking the blame for his buddies' actions, he may discover his friends stop calling him to hang out. When the employee requests a raise, she may find herself out on the curb with a cardboard box of her belongings the next morning.

When we take the blinders off that allow us only to see the good in a Mercury Mind connection, we can assess the reality of the relationship. Although this may be painful, it allows us to move toward a healthier, more satisfying connection. The nice girl can meet a man who can show he wants her without belittling her. The pushover can find friends who will hang out with him even if he doesn't do their homework for them. The employee can work for a boss who values her contributions and encourages her to have a healthy life outside of work.

It is not our responsibility to fix other people, and often, no matter what we do, we cannot force someone to change.

People Don't Change Because We Want Them To

When we see the good, bad, and ugly of the other person in the relationship, then we can take action that is in line with our own authentic attractions. However, this doesn't mean we should try to change other people. In fact, we must choose our actions with the assumption that the other person *won't* change.

Undergoing change necessitates facing uncertainty, which is something most humans hate. We won't go through this unless we are very unhappy with the current state of things. Research shows most successful changes start with a true desire to alter some deeply dissatisfactory part of ourselves.[1] The more marked the dissatisfaction, the more likely we are to change. If, conversely, we are only mildly dissatisfied, or ambivalent regarding a certain aspect of ourselves, we are unlikely to change. If our partner in the relationship isn't bothered by a certain trait in themselves, it is highly unlikely they will take steps to modify their behavior.

Dr. Ike firmly believed he did nothing wrong in his dealings with Marty. In multiple exchanges on the podcast of investigative journalist Joe Nocera, Dr. Ike defended his actions, in many cases painting himself as the victim of a man who he had done so much to help. In one of his letters he asked point-blank, "If I was so terrible, why did [Marty] stay?" By his rationale, Dr. Ike could not perceive that he was culpable for Marty's misery. Without remorse for his actions, Dr. Ike had no impetus for change. Dr. Ike was never going to be the true friend and scrupulous confidant Marty needed him to be. This therapist could change his ways no more than a leopard could rub out his spots.

This is doubly true for people who, like Dr. Ike, have toxic traits deeply interwoven with their personality and identity. People who suffer from personality disorders such as narcissism, borderline, or even obsessive-compulsive disorder are notoriously unlikely to change. Many people suffering from these conditions do not seek therapeutic intervention in their lifetime and out of those who do, many terminate therapy prematurely. For example, up to seventy percent of borderline patients leave treatment programs before completion.[2] Change is difficult and it often means admitting we made mistakes and taking responsibility for pain we might have caused. It is also terrifying to come to the conclusion that we have not been acting in alignment with our authentic selves. Addressing our fundamental characteristics could mean unraveling the very fabric of our being.

In Dr. Ike's case, he displays most of the traits for narcissistic personality disorder as outlined in the *Diagnostic and Statistical Manual of Mental Disorders*[3]. His sense of entitlement was obvious when he demanded expensive sneakers on his birthday. His flagrant need for admiration shows up in the display of framed pictures of himself standing with celebrities throughout Marty's Hampton's home. His lack of empathy was sadly evident when he couldn't even be bothered to check whether Marty was alive after his surgery. It is not in a narcissist's nature to self-reflect and critique their own behavior, because doing so would be in opposition to their pathology. Thus, Dr. Ike's likelihood of repentance in his lifetime is near zero.

Even for someone whose traits aren't pathological, their behaviors are unlikely to change if they are part of a long-standing pattern. For example, a man who starts loudly slurping soup after a recent lip surgery might be able to change that as he heals. However, a man who's been noisily narfing nosh his entire life probably isn't going to suddenly eat in silence. For the first guy, slurping is not a deeply ingrained behavior, so it is easy to change when he feels embarrassed. However, the man who is a life-long slurper obviously has gone years without changing, indicating he probably isn't too concerned about his poor manners.

When we recognize these deeply embedded characteristics, whether pathological or not, we can save ourselves substantial anguish by accepting them as immutable. If we are tethered to who we hope a person *could be* rather than who they *are*, we are working toward an unattainable goal. The narcissist will never stop making us feel small.

The compulsive worrier will not suddenly wake up and become Mr. Zen. The adventure addict will not want to settle down in a suburban homestead.

It is therefore incumbent on us to act with the knowledge that the other person in the relationship will not change by our will. Armed with this knowledge, ask whether you can honestly be happy in a relationship if the other person never changes. If your boss never stops taking credit for your accomplishments, does that relationship give you enough opportunities to build your professional career? If your friend never stops criticizing your clothes, does she give you enough support in the friendship to make it worthy of your time? If your boyfriend never stops slurping soup, does he have enough other lovable qualities to make staying worthwhile?

By prioritizing the fulfillment of our desires above the preservation of the relationship, we can honestly assess whether these unchangeable characteristics make the relationship healthy for us. We can gauge whether these traits conflict with our value systems and prevent us from satisfying our desires more than they help us to connect with our authentic selves. If the boss unceremoniously taking credit for our hard work goes against our prioritization of an ethical work environment, then this relationship conflicts with our value system. If the fact that our friend side-eyes every sundress we wear makes us feel unsupported, then our desire for a sympathetic relationship is unmet. If our boyfriend slurping his soup turns us off more than his charm and rock-hard abs turn us on, then our desire for sexual intimacy may be better served with another partner.

It is up to us to decide what we can live with and what we cannot live with. The only thing we have to accept is that what we despise now might not change in the future. While breaking up with someone because "she eats her peas one at a time" may be ridiculous to anyone but Jerry Seinfeld, if this behavior is truly intolerable to Jerry, it is a good enough reason to break off the relationship. The girl won't likely start shoveling peas by the spoonful and if he can't see the good beyond that trait, the relationship isn't worth the investment.

Most likely, our perceived Mercury Mind connections will stand the test of pea eating, but the principle of 'me first' still stands. In any relationship, at any time, if we are vigilant in evaluating whether the relationship serves us and we like serving it in the current state, then we know we are working toward our authentic selves without getting distracted by the *hope* the person will change.

Time is the Great Elucidator

Sometimes it's not obvious that a person in a relationship has toxic traits. After all, characteristics might not be so blatant as painfully pragmatic pea consumption. Many of us hide our ugly side when first meeting someone else, and it can take time for the red flags to show up. In those cases, you must do some detective work to find the characteristics that could make or break the relationship before entrenching yourself too deeply in something that doesn't serve you.

Often, in the midst of Mercury Mind fervor at the beginning of a relationship, we may miss the red flags. These potential deal breakers may be particularly hard to spot because most people are on their best behavior when they first get to know someone they like. How then can we see through the 'nice guy/gal' routine to the real person underneath?

The simplest way to find the authentic person in all of someone's imperfect humanity is through time. With time, we all return to our true natures in one way or another. As our facades crack, our real selves shine through for better or worse. If we find the person underneath the mask does not match the person we thought someone was, we then have to do the often painful work of honestly assessing whether the Mercury Mind connection still exists. If someone tried hard throughout our relationship to be someone they were not, then we don't know the real person. We know a chameleon. We may have fallen in love with the red, blue, yellow, or purple version of that person, but they will always fade back to green at some point. Can we love the chameleon in its natural green? If not, we should move on.

For many of us, the prospect of waiting it out to see someone's true colors feels like an excruciating exercise in patience. Life is short, made all the shorter by toxic relationships that suck our time, energy, and being. Most of us don't have twenty-seven years to waste on someone who can't give us what we want. Fear not, however, there is a way to see someone's chameleon green before they choose to let their guard down.

The quickest way to know how someone *will* treat you in the future is to observe how they treat the people they are closest to now. With parents, siblings, and close friends, people have already had the time to let their guard down. If your oh-so-wonderful new beau love-bombs you with compliments over your terrific turkey, but lambastes his mom over her subpar sweet potatoes, you know how he'll be treating you five years down the road. Or if your girlfriend showers you with kisses after an expensive birthday dinner, but ices out her sister after she gives her a cheap sweater as a gift, you know if you don't spend money, she'll kick your cajones to the curb. If your new mentor proclaims you're the next prodigy of the personal fitness world, yet screams at his other long-time mentees that they need to do better to be like you, it's quite probable in a few years your ears will be ringing in the wake of his wrath when he takes the next muscle-head hotshot under his wing.

Time is the great elucidator, but fortunately for us, other people have already put in the time so we don't have to.

There is one caveat to this rule of time, which is to examine current, not past, relationships as a barometer. We all make mistakes. Some of us learn, grow, and do better in subsequent relationships. It is unfair and unwise to judge your new partner by their past without giving them the benefit of the doubt. What matters is their current behavior in their current relationships, not how they may have treated someone years ago.

Common Red Flags

Now we know what it takes to uncover the red flags, what exactly are the red flags to watch out for? Obviously, these deal breakers aren't the same for every person (as evidenced by Jerry Seinfeld and his pea-fixation), but there are a few universal indicators that suggest we might be dealing with a toxic person.

They Don't Align With Your Value System

My ex and I drove through New York state smack dab in the middle of the COVID-19 pandemic. We were on our way to pick up a new car, but my ex convinced me to make a detour to the local shopping mall. This was 2020, before the vaccine came out, so stores were still operating on heavy lockdown policies and only allowing three people inside at a time. My ex strode up to the Louis Vuitton store and immediately soured as she saw the line of people waiting to get in. Instead of patiently standing in line, she stormed up to the young saleswoman at the front.

"Why do I have to wait in this line?" screamed my ex, waving her credit card in front of the girl's face, "This is ridiculous! I'm just going to buy a freakin' purse."

"Ma'am, I'm sorry for the wait," quavered the clerk, "It's simply store policy."

"What a bitch," my ex said none-too-quietly, shooting the girl daggers as she stomped off. "Louis Vuitton will never get my business again."

At that moment, I realized my ex didn't align with my value system. Not only would I never blame a sales associate for following her company guidelines in the middle of an uncertain time, but I would never blatantly disregard others who were in the exact same position as me. She wasn't more important than anyone else waiting in that line, yet she believed she was entitled to red carpet treatment.

Another way we might notice this misalignment is if someone we have a relationship with treats others differently than they do us. A co-worker screams at the waiter for accidentally forgetting to put the dressing on the side. Your friend picks a fight with your other friend for not drinking beer at the ballgame. Your dad laughs at your grandmother behind her back after she tripped and fell flat on her face.

If the person you have a relationship with is a jerk to other people, then there's a good chance they will someday be a jerk to you. Someone who mistreats others they perceive as inferior, berates the people you love, or talks trash about their own loved ones has little respect for other people. And to have a loving relationship, respect is essential.

Remember, you are "not that special," as my friend Rich says to me. If someone treats everyone else a certain way they will eventually treat you that way too. When someone flagrantly goes against your values, it often isn't a 'slip-up'. It's a glimpse of what they truly believe, and it can be a sign that this person has another side that can emerge when things don't go their way.

They Are Addicts

If someone we are attracted to is addicted to anything—alcohol, drugs, playstation, or social media, it is often an indicator they are actively trying to hide a part of themselves. The addiction allows them to escape into another world beyond the relationship. It's a separate realm where we cannot reach them.

Our conscious wants, especially when they are addictions, are simply placeholders for what we *really* want. Addiction indicates a person is unwilling to dive deep to face their authentic desires. If they can't confront their real self, they cannot knowingly share it with you. Without this ability, true intimacy will remain a pipe dream.

They Struggle to Care for their Mental Health

People with untreated, diagnosable mental disorders such as bipolar, depression, or anxiety carry baggage with them. If we are in a relationship with someone like this we need to decide whether we can handle the low-lows as well as the high-highs. It is not fair to ourselves to enter into a relationship with someone who might need extra attention from us if we are not the kind of person willing to give that attention in the first place. Or it could be that a person we feel a Mercury Mind attraction to may need space from us a week at a time in order to work through their own mental health battles.

We will need to check-in on our own mental and emotional health, as well as our self-esteem level to judge whether this kind of relationship will deplete us, or lift us up. It's possible that we may be drawn to someone who is bipolar because we are borderline and together we understand deeply what it is like to struggle with personality disorders.

Where we need to be careful is engaging in relationships with people who refuse to seek help for their mental conditions. This is a sign that they are possibly unwilling to care for themselves and may struggle with low self-esteem. If they tend to blame their flaws, such as narcissistic tendencies, violent outbursts, compulsive lying, or obsessive thought patterns on their condition, this is a person we want to avoid because they will refuse to take responsibility for their actions and themselves. We absolutely can and should have compassion for these people, but just because they have a diagnosis does not mean they aren't responsible for their actions. We can't let them use a diagnosis as an excuse to treat us poorly.

Consider Joe, who struggles with ADHD. He often forgets his scheduled dates with his girlfriend, Lucy, because he is distracted by other activities. Sometimes, he shows up an hour late. Other times, he doesn't show up at all. Lucy can be compassionate that Joe is struggling to focus, however he doesn't seem to be making any concerted effort to improve their relationship after many talks about how hurtful ditching dates is for Lucy. No one is obligated to put up with degrading behavior if they have clearly stated what they need, even if the other person has a diagnosed condition.

They Meld their Mercury Mind to Others

Take a discerning look at the quality of people someone chooses to incorporate into their life. Like a chameleon, if a person is always changing their color depending on who they are with, it is difficult to know which version of them is real. If they behave completely differently with one friend group compared to how they act with another group, that's a sign. Or if they are boisterous and warm with their family but tight-lipped and demure at brunch with their college friends, have a discussion to see which person is the real them.

Likewise, if you notice someone's friends all seem to be doing illegal activities or stirring up constant drama, it's possible that your person is the common denominator. Like gravitates toward like. If you really can't stand your new connection's friends, family, or associates, it could be a sign to jump ship.

In Their Book, You Come In Last Place (are you plan "Z"?)

Lastly, if you notice a pattern of always being put in last place, the relationship isn't healthy. Of course, in non-romantic relationships you may not always come first. But if you are important to a person you should not consistently be their last priority. For example, if your buddy always canceled beers with you to go out with his other friends, he might not be such a good pal. If your mom always calls your sister when she's sick, but never picks up the phone to check in on you, she might not value you the way you want to be valued. And if your spouse constantly puts work, the kids, and the gym ahead of a glass of wine and a good chat with you at the end of the day, then your marriage might need a reset.

While everyone should put their authentic desires at the forefront, this doesn't diminish the need to invest in the relationships we want to maintain. If we can't be bothered to prioritize the people we care about, then we are not building true connections with them. In the same vein, both parties must be open-minded to the mutual development of the relationship. If one constantly dismisses the other's need for a modicum of attention, then there is a disconnect. The people who truly love you, make you feel loved.

There are four things you need for any relationship to work—a strong Mercury Mind connection, respect, trust, and mutual vulnerability. The red flags explored in this section are all indicators that one or more of these factors may be missing from the relationship. As powerful as a Mercury Mind connection may feel, without all four factors in place, the relationship does not have a foundation of *true* love. In these situations, we are setting out for a torturous ride.

The Responsibility of Change Lies With Us

If someone's behavior is intolerable, it is time for change. However, we cannot expect them to change. We, therefore, must be the ones to change the dynamic of the relationship. To change the relationship, we have two options—end the relationship, or stay in the relationship and accept the person exactly as they are.

While setting boundaries is a tactic often touted by well-meaning friends and therapists alike, this middle ground can become a warzone for misunderstanding. Imagine the man who finds his live-in girlfriend clingy, so he tells her she can only call him once a day. The girl limits her regular ten calls to one, all the while fighting her impulse to check in more. As a result, she becomes resentful for not being allowed to be her gregarious self and the man, who can sense her eagerness even without the hourly phone calls, still feels annoyed. Soon enough, they find themselves in nightly screaming matches. If instead of setting boundaries the man had ended the relationship when he realized they both wanted different things, or accepted his girlfriend's neediness, they both would have been better off.

With this in mind, there are three steps to determining whether the best course of action is to stay or end the relationship.

Step One is to take stock of the relationship. Are you happy being around this person? Do you feel liked, loved, and respected? If you regularly tolerate toxic behavior, check in with yourself to assess why you allow it. Are you putting the relationship before your own desires? Are you allowing your evaluation of your self-worth to be based on someone else's value system or on your own?

Also, take ownership if *you* are the cause of toxicity. Your girlfriend calling you ten times a day may have an unhealthy need for attention, but if you constantly stonewall her, she has reason to feel insecure. If you torture a dog by constantly prodding it with a stick, it will bite. And you cannot blame the dog for self-defense.

Step Two is to accept that the person will not change because you want them to. The addict won't toss the wine or cocaine down the toilet if she doesn't actually want to stop drinking or snorting. Therefore, we have to assess whether *we* are willing to change. Are we willing to adjust our expectations or does the status quo go against our true desires or values? For example, we could change from nagging to joining the alcoholic in nightly binges or cocaine parties, but is that in line with what we want? Does guzzling gin or inhaling drugs go against our moral fiber?

Step Three is to ask ourselves whether we are willing to tolerate the other person if they don't change. We must ask ourselves how keeping this relationship intact impacts the pursuit of our desires. Perhaps if our boss is an alcoholic, but their drinking has little influence on our job, then we can tolerate this behavior because the experience we get from our professional relationship is more valuable than the inconvenience of a boss who smells a bit boozy in the morning. However, if our husband is an alcoholic, and his behavior actively prevents the close connection we want, then the relationship may have to end.

Ending the Relationship Doesn't Always Mean Breaking it Off

When we realize we may need to end relationships with people we are close to it can feel mean.

But hold up, I can't just cut my mom out of my life!

However, just because a relationship ends, doesn't mean we can't begin a *new* relationship with the same person. You don't have to cut your mom out of your life because she gossips a little too much. But you may need to end the relationship that involves you listening as your mom spills the beans about Aunt Susie's miscarriages twenty years ago and instead refocus the relationship so it gives you more of what you need. If you need comfort instead of gossip, this means starting a new relationship with your mom where you clearly communicate what you need at the beginning of the conversation.

"I don't need to talk about what happened to Auntie Susie right now, Mom," you might express, "I need to talk about what happened to me."

Relationships, like cycles, are a series of beginnings and endings. We are constantly on a path to creating deeper, richer relationships, and sometimes this means ending a relationship in its current form and starting afresh with a mutual commitment to a different type of connection.

To start this new connection, focus on the good qualities of the individual. Does this person bring you laughter, support, or joy? Focus on those things and start from there to build a new relationship from that foundation. If you can't find *any* good aspects of a particular relationship, that relationship may have died long ago.

Relationships should be an active process. Each year, we should reintroduce ourselves to start our cycles afresh and allow for our relationships to grow. If the connection is strong and contains the seedlings of respect, trust, and vulnerability, then it can grow despite the ice storms and high winds that are part of any relationship. We are as individuals constantly evolving and, so too, should our relationships.

Often, we tolerate toxic people in our lives because we have a deficiency of self-esteem and self-respect. Like Marty Markowitz, we fall prey to others when we try to please them at the cost of forgetting to please ourselves. But when we end our toxic relationships, we build up our self-esteem. In recognizing the toxicity in others, we acknowledge what we need and we reset our compass to prioritize our authentic desires. We cultivate the power to love our true selves, regardless of how the other person responds. And when we love ourselves with admiration, we have an incredible well of love to draw on and give to others with confidence.

.

Conclusion: The Journey Ahead

This journey is not an easy one. Discovering yourself takes courage and commitment. It helps to have loving people in your corner who can help you uncover your strengths and overcome your weaknesses. This process requires you to face the unknown head-on. Accepting yourself requires deep humility and courageous vulnerability. And living from a place of unrelenting authenticity means shouldering the burden of sometimes unbearable loneliness.

Yet, if we don't embark, we can never know the fullness of what we can truly be in this world. If we don't get real with ourselves, then relationships can remain forever shrouded in the mist of a false cloud. We become shells of ourselves, hollow mimicries that recite half-truths while our authentic selves fade to black in a forgotten corner of our hearts.

Who could you be if you weren't this person you've made up? What potentials, views, and loves await you beyond the sycophantic, societally-approved version of yourself that you've built your life around? When we look in the mirror, we must be fully honest with ourselves first.

In the BBC documentary on Kris Kristofferson[1], Johnny Cash paraphrases the words he read in a letter from Kristofferson's mother.

She wrote to him after he abandoned his prestigious military commission as an English Literature Professor at West Point to become a janitor at Columbia Records. His conservative family thought he was insane.

"You are disowned," she wrote. "You're no longer my son. You gave up your Rhodes scholarship, you gave up your education, your career, everything else that was planned for you. And you've gone to Nashville to be a bum and hang out, trying to be with people like Johnny Cash and Hank Williams. And don't ever darken my door again."

From the moment Kris Kristofferson touched down in Nashville, rubbing elbows with the likes of cowboy legend Jack Clement, he felt like he'd stepped into his true self. There was no turning back from this person he had discovered underneath the Rhodes scholar, the military man, and the family man with the high school sweetheart and the young daughter. This man at the heart of him had words boiling in his chest that would burn him to a crisp if he tried to shove them down any longer.

"I think I would have probably drunk myself to death if I hadn't got into something creative," Kristofferson once said. "I always felt like Nashville saved my life."[2]

If not for this decision to act in accordance with his truth, in spite of his mother's admonitions, we wouldn't know the wonderful words of Kris Kristofferson today. This choice was painful, lonely, and left him with Goliath-sized demons as he struggled to leave his idyllic American life behind. The dust didn't settle for many years. In one of Kristofferson's breakout hits, "Sunday Morning Coming Down," a baleful tenor sings, backed by a lively fiddle. The words are about missing out on things he thought would be in his future: a loving relationship with his family, being a dad, and a life of ease.

Kristofferson felt the weight of his choice. Yet even though he braved the heartache of leaving his old life behind, he wasn't alone forever. He went on to become one of the most iconic songwriting legends in the annals of Nashville history, garnering appointments in the Country Music Hall of Fame[3], the Songwriters Hall of Fame[4], and the Nashville Songwriters Hall of Fame.[5] He found deep enduring friendships and relationships in the Nashville community. He uncovered lyrics that could express the turmoil of a changing country and the timeless heartbreak of the human condition with honesty, grace, and compassion. His words have echoed over the radio waves for generations, and will continue to do so for many decades to come.

Your authenticity can bring you into a space of freedom and joy too, and it will attract Mercury Mind connections with others who share and appreciate your eccentricities.

Building Yourself Into Yourself

Embracing your Mercury Mind is about learning to live comfortably in your own skin. When we see, accept, and pursue our honest attractions, we create an intimate relationship with our authentic selves. We love ourselves again. Moreover, by pursuing this journey, we give others the opportunity to love the real us, perhaps for the first time.

The biggest key to connecting with the Mercury Mind is to make our authentic subconscious wants more conscious and remove the shame surrounding our genuine desires. When we can identify our authentic attractions we can remove the roadblocks in our way and take healthy action in pursuit of our true wants. We can see people for who they are and what they bring to our lives, not who we want them to be. We can walk up the mountain, trusting with each step that we are moving toward where we want to be, even if we don't know precisely where the path will lead. We know the great and joyful rewards of true connections, and the physical, emotional, and psychological consequences of shallow relationships. Ultimately, we can learn to work *with* our Mercury Mind, as it inexplicably drives us into all-consuming passions, lighting fires and burning bridges without discretion. We can act from this Mercury Mind to create, rather than destroy.

This path is possible. More than that, like Kris Kristofferson, by walking down it, we all have a chance, a grand opportunity, to be someone great, whatever form this person comes in.

The question now is will you choose to walk down this road, or will you continue to play it small? Will you live your life accepting less of yourself, or will you dare to be great?

If you ever feel like you've come to a standstill on this journey, reopen the cycle. Step into the unknown. Stillness is an illusion we create. If we are open to walking forward, the path will rise to meet us. The road forward already exists, we just need to trust that we'll find it.

When you feel stuck, remind yourself there is always a deeper question to ask. If you find yourself saying, "Ugh, I'm stuck in this dead-end job, with this horrid girlfriend, in this flyover town," try asking yourself, "Why am I here in this town? What do I get out of this job? What does my girlfriend give to me that I want?" From there, you'll find the nuggets of your authentic desires lying behind your unsatisfying conscious plans, and you can use these as guideposts to the life you want.

The life we desire is there, all we have to do is *ask* to uncover it. By asking about what we want, we take a step closer to getting it.

The Lonely Road

When you choose the road of authenticity, you choose to step off the worn path. You will wander off the packed dirt into the bramble bushes and weeds of the unknown.

It is not easy. We will scrape our legs and our knees. We will draw blood. We will leave our companions behind when they decide to wander back to the comfort of the trail, leaving only footprints as a memory.

This path is a lonely one. It demands vulnerability, honest reflection, and an almost inhuman ability to persist in the face of doubt. It requires shedding our human dislike of the unknown and settling into cycles we cannot control or predict. And in the face of this uncertain and painful route, we must have faith that, when we do follow our authentic desires and cultivate our intimate relationship with ourselves, our life will unfold with meaning and purpose. This road demands trust, even though sometimes it seems like it has no right to do so.

However, walking this road does get easier with time. Like any pursuit worth its salt, accepting ourselves in our raw form and actively living from this space takes practice. Like learning to ride a bike, or figuring out how to French kiss, or stumbling our way to a degree in astrophysics, practice does make it better. With effort, it soon feels more natural to embrace our true selves than it does to hide who we honestly are.

This is a life-long journey. There is no need to get it right the first, second, or even fiftieth time around. Most of us will mess up on this journey and there is nothing wrong with that. The point is not to get it perfect, but to begin a different way of living, so from here on out we can begin to live our lives as ourselves and *not* the person we've spent decades trying to be.

When you look at your life a year, two years, or ten years down the line and you feel a true connection with yourself, the people in your life, and the world around you, it will be worth it. Kris Kristofferson is living proof. You will find a wonderful being inside of you. Questioning yourself and opening your cycles will eventually unveil a deeper level of your soul.

Right now, this journey may seem daunting. It should be scary. It requires you to upend your life and go out into the wild, beyond where most humans dare to go. But it's just one step followed by another. Rinse and repeat until one day you'll find yourself at the top of the mountain without even remembering quite how you managed to get there. And wow, the air is thin at the top. And the view is incredible.

But to get there you must *start*. Because if you don't, you'll never reach the peak. Without the struggle you'll never be free enough to breathe that rarified air and take in that glorious, unencumbered vista.

On his tombstone, Kris Kristofferson requested three lines from Leonard Cohen be engraved[6]: "Like a bird on a wire / Like a drunk in a midnight choir / I have tried in my own way to be free." Kristofferson is free. He worked to become free and it gave him a real life.

If you begin right now, in this moment, you too can be free. As

Kristofferson says in his song "Me and Bobby McGee," "Freedom is just another word for nothing left to lose."

We all have to face a question one day. As our journey comes to an end will we say, "I'm glad I did" or "I wish I did"?

So….What do you have to lose?

Notes

Introduction: Relationships Matter More than we Think

1. Cottrell, Sarah. "This Mom Lifted a Car off Her Trapped Child. and so Can You." Medium. Medium, January 23, 2021. https://sarahcottrell.medium.com/this-mom-lifted-a-car-off-her-trapped-child-and-so-can-you-8e13d6223863.
2. "Mother Fights off Polar Bear to Save Children | CBC News." CBCnews. CBC/Radio Canada, February 10, 2006. https://www.cbc.ca/news/canada/mother-fights-off-polar-bear-to-save-children-1.625164.
3. ComicBook. "The Incredible Hulk's Creation Was Inspired by a Woman Saving a Child." Comicbook.com. Comicbook.com. Accessed February 11, 2022. https://comicbook.com/news/the-incredible-hulks-creation-was-inspired-by-a-woman-saving-a-c/.
4. Wright, George. "NXIVM: 'Why I Joined a Cult - and How I Left'." BBC News. BBC, April 13, 2019. https://www.bbc.com/news/world-47900242.
5. Humphreys, C. "Mental Health and Domestic Violence: 'I Call It Symptoms of Abuse'." *British Journal of Social Work*33, no. 2 (2003): 209–26. https://doi.org/10.1093/bjsw/33.2.209.
6. "Effects of Violence against Women." Effects of violence against women | Office on Women's Health. Accessed February 12, 2022. https://www.womenshealth.gov/relationships-and-safety/effects-violence-against-women.
7. Fuller-Thomson, Esme, and Sarah Brennenstuhl. "Making a Link between Childhood Physical Abuse and Cancer." *Cancer* 115, no. 14 (2009): 3341–50. https://doi.org/10.1002/cncr.24372.
8. Marmot, M. G.; Rose, G.; Shipley, M.; Hamilton, P. J. (1978). "Employment grade and coronary heart disease in British civil servants". *Journal of Epidemiology and Community Health*. **32** (4): 244–249.
9. Barnett, Rosalind Chait, Andrew Steptoe, and Karen C. Gareis. "Marital-Role Quality and Stress-Related Psychobiological Indicators." *Annals of Behavioral Medicine* 30, no. 1 (2005): 36–43. https://doi.org/10.1207/s15324796abm3001_5.
10. Rhoades, Galena K., Claire M. Kamp Dush, David C. Atkins, Scott M. Stanley, and Howard J. Markman. "Breaking up Is Hard to Do: The Impact of Unmarried Relationship Dissolution on Mental Health and Life Satisfaction." *Journal of Family Psychology* 25, no. 3 (2011): 366–74. https://doi.org/10.1037/a0023627.
11. Stockman, J.A. "The Spread of Obesity in a Large Social Network over 32 Years." *Yearbook of Pediatrics* 2009 (2009): 464–66. https://doi.org/10.1016/s0084-3954(08)79134-6.
12. Al-Kandari, Yagoub Yousif, and Maha Meshari Al-Sejari. "Social Isolation, Social Support and Their Relationship with Smartphone Addiction." *Information, Communication & Society* 24, no. 13 (2020): 1925–43. https://doi.org/10.1080/1369118x.2020.1749698.
13. Christie, Nina C. "The Role of Social Isolation in Opioid Addiction." *Social Cognitive and Affective Neuroscience*, 2021. https://doi.org/10.1093/scan/nsab029.

Notes

14. Wang, Yun-He, Jin-Qiao Li, Ju-Fang Shi, Jian-Yu Que, Jia-Jia Liu, Julia M. Lappin, Janni Leung, et al. "Depression and Anxiety in Relation to Cancer Incidence and Mortality: A Systematic Review and Meta-Analysis of Cohort Studies." *Molecular Psychiatry* 25, no. 7 (2019): 1487–99. https://doi.org/10.1038/s41380-019-0595-x.
15. Mirror.co.uk. "Falling in Love Saved My Life." mirror, February 21, 2012. https://www.mirror.co.uk/lifestyle/sex-relationships/falling-love-saved-life-699903.
16. "Romantic Love : Can It Last?" Helen Fisher PhD. Accessed February 9, 2022. https://helenfisher.com/romantic-love-can-it-last/.
17. Acevedo, Bianca P., Arthur Aron, Helen E. Fisher, and Lucy L. Brown. "Neural Correlates of Long-Term Intense Romantic Love." *Social Cognitive and Affective Neuroscience* 7, no. 2 (2011): 145–59. https://doi.org/10.1093/scan/nsq092.
18. Wood, Robert G., Sarah Avellar, and Brian Goesling. *The Effects of Marriage on Health a Synthesis of Recent Research Evidence.* New York: Nova Science, 2009.
19. "Marriage Linked to Lower Heart Risks in Study of 3.5+ Million Adults." American College of Cardiology, March 28, 2014. https://www.acc.org/about-acc/press-releases/2014/03/28/09/55/alviar-marital-status.
20. Grundström, Jenna, Hanna Konttinen, Noora Berg, and Olli Kiviruusu. "Associations between Relationship Status and Mental Well-Being in Different Life Phases from Young to Middle Adulthood." *SSM - Population Health* 14 (2021): 100774. https://doi.org/10.1016/j.ssmph.2021.100774.
21. Roelfs, David J., Eran Shor, Rachel Kalish, and Tamar Yogev. "The Rising Relative Risk of Mortality for Singles: Meta-Analysis and Meta-Regression." *American Journal of Epidemiology* 174, no. 4 (2011): 379–89. https://doi.org/10.1093/aje/kwr111.
22. King, Kathleen B., and Harry T. Reis. "Marriage and Long-Term Survival after Coronary Artery Bypass Grafting." *Health Psychology* 31, no. 1 (2012): 55–62. https://doi.org/10.1037/a0025061.
23. Holt-lunstad, Julianne, and Timothy Smith. "Social Relationships and Mortality Risk: A Meta-Analytic Review." *SciVee*, 2010. https://doi.org/10.4016/19911.01.
24. Yang, Yang Claire, Courtney Boen, Karen Gerken, Ting Li, Kristen Schorpp, and Kathleen Mullan Harris. "Social Relationships and Physiological Determinants of Longevity across the Human Life Span." *Proceedings of the National Academy of Sciences* 113, no. 3 (2016): 578–83. https://doi.org/10.1073/pnas.1511085112.
25. Penninkilampi, Ross, Anne-Nicole Casey, Maria Fiatarone Singh, and Henry Brodaty. "The Association between Social Engagement, Loneliness, and Risk of Dementia: A Systematic Review and Meta-Analysis." *Journal of Alzheimer's Disease* 66, no. 4 (2018): 1619–33. https://doi.org/10.3233/jad-180439.
26. Kernis, Michael H., and Brian M. Goldman. "A Multicomponent Conceptualization of Authenticity: Theory and Research." *Advances in Experimental Social Psychology*, 2006, 283–357. https://doi.org/10.1016/s0065-2601(06)38006-9.

1. We Don't Know what We Want

1. Fisher, Helen E. *Why We Love: The Nature and Chemistry of Romantic Love.* New York: St. Martin's Griffin, 2005.
2. Gottman, John, and Julie Gottman. "The Natural Principles of Love." *Journal of Family Theory & Review* 9, no. 1 (2017): 7–26. https://doi.org/10.1111/jftr.12182.

2. Closing Uncertain Cycles

1. MORAN, EMILIO F. *Human Adaptability: An Introduction to Ecological Anthropology.* S.l.: ROUTLEDGE, 2022.
2. "Mental Health." World Health Organization. World Health Organization. Accessed December 8, 2021. https://www.who.int/health-topics/mental-health.
3. "Over 95% of the World's Population Has Health Problems, with over a Third Having More than Five Ailments." ScienceDaily. ScienceDaily, June 8, 2015. https://www.sciencedaily.com/releases/2015/06/150608081753.htm.
4. Elizabeth, De. "Why Uncertainty Feels so Terrifying, and How to Cope with It." HuffPost. HuffPost, March 9, 2021. https://www.huffpost.com/entry/uncertainty-stress-how-to-cope_l_5ed0047cc5b6521c93a80e43.
5. Kruglanski, Arie W., and Donna M. Webster. "Motivated Closing of the Mind: 'Seizing' and 'Freezing'.'' *Psychological Review* 103, no. 2 (1996): 263–83. https://doi.org/10.1037/0033-295x.103.2.263.
6. Macur, Juliet. "Simone Biles and the Weight of Perfection." The New York Times. The New York Times, July 24, 2021. https://www.nytimes.com/2021/07/24/sports/olympics/simone-biles-gymnastics.html.
7. "'The Cat Got Fed Instead of Us': Simone Biles Discusses Her Childhood Hunger." The Guardian. Guardian News and Media, June 30, 2021. https://www.the-guardian.com/sport/2021/jun/30/simone-biles-foster-care-adoption-grandparents-gymnastics.
8. "When Did Simone Biles Start Her Gymnastics Journey?" EssentiallySports, October 14, 2021. https://www.essentiallysports.com/us-sports-news-gymnastics-news-when-did-simone-biles-start-her-gymnastics-journey/.
9. "Simone Biles: Athlete of the Year 2021." Time. Time. Accessed December 9, 2021. https://time.com/athlete-of-the-year-2021-simone-biles/.
10. Chang, Rachel. "How the BTK Killer Got His Name - and the Paper Trail He Left Behind." Biography.com. A&E Networks Television, July 6, 2021. https://www.biography.com/news/btk-killer-meaning-dennis-rader-clues.
11. "Serial Killer, Who Dressed up as His Victims, Has Done a Tell-All Interview." news. news.com.au - Australia's leading news site, September 4, 2018. https://www.news.com.au/world/north-america/kansas-btk-serial-killer-dennis-rader-said-a-demon-within-me-made-him-murder/news-story/9ff3d7a3d55-fa5044812f050b2332a28.
12. Baranova, Ivanna, and Domenica Martinello. *Confirmation Bias.* Montreal, Quebec: Metatron Press, 2019.
13. "The Capitol Riots, Qanon, and the Internet." https://iddp.gwu.edu. Accessed December 10, 2021. https://iddp.gwu.edu/capitol-riots-qanon-and-internet.
14. Bleakley, Paul. "Panic, Pizza and Mainstreaming the Alt-Right: A Social Media Analysis of Pizzagate and the Rise of the Qanon Conspiracy." *Current Sociology*, 2021, 001139212110348. https://doi.org/10.1177/00113921211034896.
15. Sophia Moskalenko Research Fellow in Social Psychology. "Many Qanon Followers Report Having Mental Health Diagnoses." The Conversation, November 24, 2021. https://theconversation.com/many-qanon-followers-report-having-mental-health-diagnoses-157299.
16. Noor, Iqra. "Confirmation Bias." Confirmation Bias | Simply Psychology, June 10, 2020. https://www.simplypsychology.org/confirmation-bias.html.
17.

Notes

3. Self-Confidence Trap

1. Carnegie, Dale. *How to Win Friends and Influence People*. S.l.: SIMON & SCHUSTER, 1936.
2. "3 Rules for Texting Girls (Make Her Chase You!) - Youtube." Accessed December 14, 2021. https://www.youtube.com/watch?v=V0vimFiUKQQ.
3. Shuter, Robert, and Sumana Chattopadhyay. "Emerging Interpersonal Norms of Text Messaging in India and the United States." *Journal of Intercultural Communication Research* 39, no. 2 (2010): 123–47. https://doi.org/10.1080/17475759.2010.526319.

4. Building Authentic Self-Esteem

1. Mischel, Walter; Ebbesen, Ebbe B. (1970). "Attention in delay of gratification". *Journal of Personality and Social Psychology*. **16** (2): 329–337
2. Tangney, June P., Angie Luzio Boone, and Roy F. Baumeister. "High Self-Control Predicts Good Adjustment, Less Pathology, Better Grades, and Interpersonal Success." *Self-Regulation and Self-Control,* 2018, 173–212. https://doi.org/10.4324/9781315175775-5.
3. Block, Jennifer A, Elizabeth Santa Ana, Monica L Rodriguez, and Melissa Colsman. "Delay of Gratification: Impulsive Choices and Problem Behaviors in Early and Late Adolescence." *Journal of Personality* 70, no. 4 (2002): 533–52. https://doi.org/10.1111/1467-6494.05013.
4. Ho, Shi-Yun, Eddie M. Tong, and Lile Jia. "Authentic and Hubristic Pride: Differential Effects on Delay of Gratification." *Emotion* 16, no. 8 (2016): 1147–56. https://doi.org/10.1037/emo0000179.
5. Cheng, Ying-Yao, Paichi Pat Shein, and Wen-Bin Chiou. "Escaping the Impulse to Immediate Gratification: The Prospect Concept Promotes a Future-Oriented Mindset, Prompting an Inclination towards Delayed Gratification." *British Journal of Psychology* 103, no. 1 (2011): 129–41. https://doi.org/10.1111/j.2044-8295.2011.02067.x.
6. Kenny, Anthony, and Charles Kenny. *Life, Liberty, and the Pursuit of Utility: Happiness in Philosophical and Economic Thought*. Exeter: Imprint Academic, 2006.

5. Finding True Connection in Relationships

1. Chandler, David. *The Campaigns of Napoleon*. London: Weidenfeld & Nicolson, 1995.
2. Durant, Will. *The Age of Napoleon*. New York: Simon & Schuster, 1975.
3. McLynn, Frank. *Napoleon: A Biography*. New York: Arcade Pub., 1997.
4. Roberts, Andrew. *Napoleon: A Life*. New York, NY: Penguin Books, 2015.
5. Zamoyski, Adam. "The Personality Traits That Led to Napoleon Bonaparte's Epic Downfall." History.com. A&E Television Networks, January 4, 2019. https://www.history.com/news/napoleon-bonaparte-downfall-reasons-personality-traits.
6. "The (Sexist) Napoleonic Code Was Established in 1804." Star, March 24, 2019. https://www.tribstar.com/features/valley_life/the-sexist-napoleonic-code-was-established-in-1804/article_bffad258-1c54-567b-9c72-b2b90452b76b.html.

7. Parker, Harold T. "The Formation of Napoleon's Personality: An Exploratory Essay." *French Historical Studies* 7, no. 1 (1971): 6. https://doi.org/10.2307/286104.
8. "Zach Galifianakis Stand-up | Late Night with Conan O'Brien." *YouTube*, YouTube, 28 Oct. 2019, https://www.youtube.com/watch?v=0Tk9k-5zd5k.
9. "Zach Galifianakis Believes Bullies Just Need Love." *YouTube*, YouTube, 3 Nov. 2020, https://www.youtube.com/watch?v=mPCrLfwC3SQ.

6. Step One, Identifying Our Attractions

1. Ando, Hironori, Kazuyoshi Ukena, and Shinji Nagata. *Handbook of Hormones*. London: Elsevier, Academic Press, 2021.
2. "Chronic Stress Puts Your Health at Risk." Mayo Clinic. Mayo Foundation for Medical Education and Research, July 8, 2021. https://www.mayoclinic.org/healthy-lifestyle/stress-management/in-depth/stress/art-20046037.
3. Aschbacher, Kirstin, Aoife O'Donovan, Owen M. Wolkowitz, Firdaus S. Dhabhar, Yali Su, and Elissa Epel. "Good Stress, Bad Stress and Oxidative Stress: Insights from Anticipatory Cortisol Reactivity." *Psychoneuroendocrinology* 38, no. 9 (2013): 1698–1708. https://doi.org/10.1016/j.psyneuen.2013.02.004.
4. Schoorlemmer, R. M., G. M. Peeters, N. M. van Schoor, and P. Lips. "Relationships between Cortisol Level, Mortality and Chronic Diseases in Older Persons." *Clinical Endocrinology* 71, no. 6 (2009): 779–86. https://doi.org/10.1111/j.1365-2265.2009.03552.x.
5. Balters, Stephanie, Joseph W. Geeseman, Ann-Kristin Tveten, Hans Petter Hildre, Wendy Ju, and Martin Steinert. "Mayday, Mayday, Mayday: Using Salivary Cortisol to Detect Distress (and Eustress!) in Critical Incident Training." *International Journal of Industrial Ergonomics* 78 (2020): 102975. https://doi.org/10.1016/j.ergon.2020.102975.
6. Ingraham, Christopher. "Americans Are Getting More Miserable, and There's Data to Prove It." The Washington Post. WP Company, March 22, 2019. https://www.washingtonpost.com/business/2019/03/22/americans-are-getting-more-miserable-theres-data-prove-it/.
7. "GBD Compare." Data Visualizations. Accessed January 6, 2022. https://vizhub.healthdata.org/gbd-compare/.
8. "The Lancet: Latest Global Disease Estimates Reveal Perfect Storm of Rising Chronic Diseases and Public Health Failures Fuelling COVID-19 Pandemic." Institute for Health Metrics and Evaluation, November 21, 2020. https://www.healthdata.org/news-release/lancet-latest-global-disease-estimates-reveal-perfect-storm-rising-chronic-diseases-and.
9. Balters, Stephanie, Joseph W. Geeseman, Ann-Kristin Tveten, Hans Petter Hildre, Wendy Ju, and Martin Steinert. "Mayday, Mayday, Mayday: Using Salivary Cortisol to Detect Distress (and Eustress!) in Critical Incident Training." *International Journal of Industrial Ergonomics* 78 (2020): 102975. https://doi.org/10.1016/j.ergon.2020.102975.
10. Lindfors, Petra, and Ulf Lundberg. "Is Low Cortisol Release an Indicator of Positive Health?" *Stress and Health* 18, no. 4 (2002): 153–60. https://doi.org/10.1002/smi.942.
11. Simmons, Bret L., and Debra L. Nelson. "Eustress at Work: The Relationship between Hope and Health in Hospital Nurses." *Health Care Management Review* 26, no. 4 (2001): 7–18. https://doi.org/10.1097/00004010-200110000-00002.

12. Crum, Alia J., Peter Salovey, and Shawn Achor. "Rethinking Stress: The Role of Mindsets in Determining the Stress Response." *Journal of Personality and Social Psychology* 104, no. 4 (2013): 716–33. https://doi.org/10.1037/a0031201.

13. Fisher, Helen E. *Why We Love: The Nature and Chemistry of Romantic Love*. New York: St. Martin's Griffin, 2005.

14. Cristol, Hope. "Dopamine: What It Is & What It Does." WebMD. WebMD. Accessed January 7, 2022. https://www.webmd.com/mental-health/what-is-dopamine.

15. Hormone. "Norepinephrine." Hormone Health Network. Hormone, September 4, 2019. https://www.hormone.org/your-health-and-hormones/glands-and-hormones-a-to-z/hormones/norepinephrine.

16. MARAZZITI, D., H. S. AKISKAL, A. ROSSI, and G. B. CASSANO. "Alteration of the Platelet Serotonin Transporter in Romantic Love." *Psychological Medicine* 29, no. 3 (1999): 741–45. https://doi.org/10.1017/s0033291798007946.

17. Hormone. "Serotonin." Serotonin | Hormone Health Network. Hormone, August 6, 2020. https://www.hormone.org/your-health-and-hormones/glands-and-hormones-a-to-z/hormones/serotonin.

7. Step Two, Releasing Our Conscious Attractions

1. Hamzelou, Jessica. "Clinic 'Turkey Baster' Method May Be Worth Trying before IVF." New Scientist. New Scientist, July 28, 2017. https://www.newscientist.com/article/2141985-clinic-turkey-baster-method-may-be-worth-trying-before-ivf/.

2. Moieni, Mona, and Naomi I Eisenberger. "Social Isolation and Health," 2020. https://doi.org/10.1377/hpb20200622.253235.

3. Pancani, Luca, Marco Marinucci, Nicolas Aureli, and Paolo Riva. "Forced Social Isolation and Mental Health: A Study on 1006 Italians under Covid-19 Lockdown," 2021. https://doi.org/10.31234/osf.io/uacfj.

4. Peçanha, Tiago, Karla Fabiana Goessler, Hamilton Roschel, and Bruno Gualano. "Social Isolation during the COVID-19 Pandemic Can Increase Physical Inactivity and the Global Burden of Cardiovascular Disease." *American Journal of Physiology-Heart and Circulatory Physiology* 318, no. 6 (2020). https://doi.org/10.1152/ajpheart.00268.2020.

5. Kross, E., M. G. Berman, W. Mischel, E. E. Smith, and T. D. Wager. "Social Rejection Shares Somatosensory Representations with Physical Pain." *Proceedings of the National Academy of Sciences* 108, no. 15 (2011): 6270–75. https://doi.org/10.1073/pnas.1102693108.

6. Wei, Zhenyu, Zhiying Zhao, and Yong Zheng. "Following the Majority: Social Influence in Trusting Behavior." *Frontiers in Neuroscience* 13 (2019). https://doi.org/10.3389/fnins.2019.00089.

7. Bardon, Adrian. *The Truth about Denial: Bias and Self-Deception in Science, Politics, and Religion*. New York, NY: Oxford University Press, 2020.

8. Bolsen, Toby, James N. Druckman, and Fay Lomax Cook. "Citizens', Scientists', and Policy Advisors' Beliefs about Global Warming." *The ANNALS of the American Academy of Political and Social Science* 658, no. 1 (2015): 271–95. https://doi.org/10.1177/0002716214558393.

9. Josephs, Lawrence, Benjamin Warach, Kirby L. Goldin, Peter K. Jonason, Bernard S. Gorman, Sanya Masroor, and Nixza Lebron. "Be Yourself: Authenticity as a

Long-Term Mating Strategy." *Personality and Individual Differences* 143 (2019): 118–27. https://doi.org/10.1016/j.paid.2019.02.020.

8. Step Three, Embracing Our True Attractions

1. MaharishiUniversity. "Jim Carrey at Miu: Commencement Address at the 2014 Graduation (EN, FR, Es, Ru, Gr,...)." YouTube. YouTube, May 30, 2014. https://www.youtube.com/watch?v=V80-gPkpH6M.
2. Caporal, Jack. "Here's Why 20% of Americans Have Changed Careers since the Pandemic Began." The Motley Fool. The Motley Fool, October 19, 2021. https://www.fool.com/research/20-percent-americans-changed-careers/.
3. Angell, Melissa. "There's No Slowing the Great Resignation." Inc.com. Inc., January 6, 2022. https://www.inc.com/melissa-angell/great-resignation-hits-new-record-november-jobs.html.
4. LondonRealTV. "Ivana Chubbuck on Jim Carrey | London Real." YouTube. YouTube, April 27, 2015. https://www.youtube.com/watch?v=KQHYmo0jHPE.
5. Caporal, Jack. "Here's Why 20% of Americans Have Changed Careers since the Pandemic Began." The Motley Fool. The Motley Fool, October 19, 2021. https://www.fool.com/research/20-percent-americans-changed-careers/.
6. "Projection." GoodTherapy.org Therapy Blog. Accessed January 20, 2022. https://www.goodtherapy.org/blog/psychpedia/projection.
7. Carvajal, Edduin. "Ian McKellen Came out in 1988 during a Radio Discussion - inside His Inspiring Story." news.amomama.com. news.amomama.com, November 4, 2021. https://news.amomama.com/258626-ian-mckellens-inspiring-coming-out-story.html.
8. Lang, Frieder R., and Laura L. Carstensen. "Time Counts: Future Time Perspective, Goals, and Social Relationships." *Psychology and Aging* 17, no. 1 (2002): 125–39. https://doi.org/10.1037/0882-7974.17.1.125.

9. Healthy Actions Inspire Healthy Relationships

1. Cox, Daniel A., and Brent Orrell. "Peer Pressure, Not Politics, May Matter Most When It Comes to Getting the Covid-19 Vaccine." The Survey Center on American Life, June 29, 2021. https://www.americansurveycenter.org/commentary/peer-pressure-not-politics-may-matter-most-when-it-comes-to-getting-the-covid-19-vaccine/.
2. Maslin, Janet. "The Muse Who Made the Guitars Gently Weep." The New York Times. The New York Times, August 27, 2007. https://www.nytimes.com/2007/08/27/books/27masl.html.
3. Lemmon, Valerie A., and J. Scott Mizes. "Effectiveness of Exposure Therapy: A Case Study of Posttraumatic Stress Disorder and Mental Retardation." *Cognitive and Behavioral Practice* 9, no. 4 (2002): 317–23. https://doi.org/10.1016/s1077-7229(02)80026-8.

10. The Other Person In the Relationship

1. Hudson, Nathan W., and R. Chris Fraley. "Changing for the Better? Longitudinal Associations between Volitional Personality Change and Psychological Well-Being." *Personality and Social Psychology Bulletin* 42, no. 5 (2016): 603–15. https://doi.org/10.1177/0146167216637840.
2. "Personality Disorders--Treatment for the 'Untreatable'." Monitor on Psychology. American Psychological Association. Accessed February 3, 2022. https://www.apa.org/monitor/mar04/treatment.
3. *Diagnostic and Statistical Manual of Mental Disorders: DSM-5.* Arlington, VA: American Psychiatric Association, 2017.

Conclusion: The Journey Ahead

1. Earle, Steve. "For the Good Times - The Kris Kristofferson Story." Episode. BBC, n.d.
2. "What It Takes: Wintertime in Nashville." Steven Pressfield | Website of author and historian, Steven Pressfield., July 6, 2011. https://stevenpressfield.com/2011/07/wintertime-in-nashville/.
3. "Kris Kristofferson: Artist Bio." Country Music Hall of Fame. Accessed February 5, 2022. https://countrymusichalloffame.org/artist/kris-kristofferson/.
4. "Kris Kristofferson." Kris Kristofferson | Songwriters Hall of Fame. Accessed February 5, 2022. https://www.songhall.org/profile/Kris_Kristofferson.
5. Nashville Songwriters Hall of Fame. Accessed February 5, 2022. http://nashvillesongwritersfoundation.com.s164288.gridserver.com/Site/inductee?entry_id=2186.
6. Contributor, Guest, Kevin J. Coyne, and Paul W Dennis. "Kris Kristofferson." Country Universe, February 12, 2009. http://www.countryuniverse.net/2008/08/30/songwriter-series-kris-kristofferson/.

Made in the USA
Monee, IL
20 June 2022